SELFIE

A REAL STORY

ELISA IAKOVIDOU

FATEFUL BIRTHDATE

I was born on a halcyon day in January. It was Saturday, shortly after midnight.

My spectacular passage in life had begun!

Mediums from all over the world gathered together to foretell the future of the new-born baby, me. To predict my fate! Unfortunately, all the retrograde planets gathered together right at the time of my birth. That's why I was assigned my fate! Oh, God!

I was born at the maternity clinic of Saint Helen in Athens, which still exists, now renovated for red-cheeky and healthy babies, for happy and innocent young mothers.

"God bless you, my red lobster," the doctor said to me, just because I was so flushed with exertion upon my emergence. Exertion was the only alternative to drowning. Witnessing such determination, I suppose that's why he spat three times on my face, according to our customs, to kick away the evil eye.

Ftoo, ftoo, ftoo...!

We are a bit superstitious in my country..!

I looked red-cheeked and furious just because I did not wish to emerge into an unfair world I somehow already hated. The dummy doctor brought me out anyway. I had been so happy there for nine months, floating in that fluid, listening to the beautiful sounds of music while all the time mesmerized by the intense colors. I was a happy fetus, and I felt so at home. I was hesitant to move, to change my life, to face the hostile world. I simply did not want to come out. That's all!

You unscrupulous doctor!

I was christened at home because I had a terrible cold and I was not allowed to be out of the house and was given the non-Christian name "Zavolia[1]." Maria, my godmother, spilled Christian oil all over me and then she spat on me, cursed me, and promptly left. Many years later when I was already in my middies I met her. Given how stingy she was, I wondered if she had bought the jeweled golden cross for me according to the custom. Maria was the daughter of a priest to which my mother used to say "Daughter of a priest, grandchild of the devil."

That's why I became a small devil, a demon!

I was the second child in the family. First came my brother who, like all first born babies, garnered the sympathy and love of everybody in the family. Three years later I came into the world– a red-cheeked baby with blond curls– who promptly became seriously ill. I unwittingly displaced the focus of the attention his position in the birth-order had afforded him. Severely ill. Scarcely avoiding death only because my parents stood by me with intense medical treatment and love, like big mountains beside a rocky knoll. Love heals everything; the best medicine for all diseases.

---

[1] The word comes from the Greek vocabulary and stands for a trouble maker and teaser though not devilish and mean.

Me, again on the stage. Struck by fate! Be ready for the cameras! Click!

The only problem though was that the baby didn't jump anymore and it couldn't run. It learned to live with the problem just because it was a kid and the kids forget very fast and want to run after life, to enjoy it. To have fun and jump with one good leg and one lame leg, running, limping and laughing, gay and happy.

Mostly kitsch! Eh!

It was a happy child who wanted to remain happy; but then there was the braced leg that compelled the onlooker to remind it that it was something different. A spectacular sight to see! An uncorrected error from which all eyes should be averted. A terrible mistake!

"Mama, look at that poor child, how it's walking! Why, mama, what happened to it? Who did that?"

"The God, my love."

"Why mama, the God? What has it done?"

"Very simple, it didn't behave well, it never listened to its parents' counsel. It was very disobedient. It repeatedly lied to cover its evil deeds. It didn't eat all its food and was complaining all the time, amongst much more. So watch out, it may happen to you as well if you don't behave well."

"No, mama, I don't want to become like that. I will be a good and obedient child."

"You still have time to choose a better path."

"Will it ever become well?"

"It depends on its behavior. It may then receive God's mercy and get well again. That's why we have to pray to God all time lest he somehow becomes angry and punishes us."

"I don't want to be punished; that's why I'll do whatever you say, mama!"

The poor child started crying. In the days that followed she seemed to have suffered a horrific shock as a result of the pitiful sight to which she had been exposed. Me!

A big foul! No, no, it's a penalty!

The referee has whistled!

My parents were ready to collapse and die. My mother had a nervous breakdown and my father suffered for a while from depression. They overcame their personal problems though and they stood by the "problem" at hand. Over time I became the center of everybody's love and care, and my poor brother lost everything, all his privileges; he too was only a child that increasingly longed for the love, care and affection he had once commanded. That's why he found a nest and shelter in our grandmother's arms. He nested there. Babis was her name.

His main wish was probably to "tear me out."

You can't be at war with your own blood. Love wins!

At the time I didn't understand it all. It took me many years to comprehend his behavior and come to my own resolutions. The only thing I cared for then was that I – selfie– opened all the doors to my most ardent desires. I became a spoiled child. It hurts me now even to think about it, but I wasn't me to blame, not even my parents. Their sensitivity to my problem split us apart, separated us, created a gap between us, a distance which we slowly bridged when we grew up. It wasn't because of a lack of love but rather because they set priorities with respect to me that were hurtful to my brother.

"I want a bicycle," my brother said.

"You have to wait, your sister comes first because of her leg. She needs that more."

His wishes always came second. At the time I thought that he hated me. Then...

Now, we love each other because we know...

Our mother dressed both of us very neat, tidy and clean with well sewn and cute second-hand clothes. Being a seamstress she made us look like young models. America, America the originator of second-hand clothes, discarded by rich children who threw them in the garbage. My father's sister in America, Irene, picked them up, washed them, and sent them to Greece in the years following the war.

What a party was thrown when a package from America came! We all gathered around the Pandora's box and we took out one by one all the gifts and miracles.

Both at school and in the neighborhood I was envied just because I was a beautiful, smart child with blond curls, green eyes, red lips and cheeks, clean and well-dressed. But they soothed their jealousy with my handicap and disability. This is how things always function in life. Power but pain. Love but hate, Beauty but handicap. The one completes the other. The balance of the losses! That fascinating balance of the great odds and contrasts.

I had started calling people names and swearing like a truck driver since early age. My first words were obscenities. Everybody sealed their ears and pretended they hadn't heard me every time I opened my dirty mouth.

"You act like a beast attacking people with nasty words," my uncle Yiannis said to me.

"Pff, pfff, Anthoula, you stink," said Fotis, the other brother of my mother.

"Shut up," my brother said.

"My little night pot," joked a good friend.

"I will send you to the reform school," shouted my mother, while pushing me to the corner so as to rinse my foul mouth out with black pepper.

When I had escaped her grasp and washed my burning tongue, I took revenge by swearing at her: "You ugly witch, do you think you are better than me? Eh? I learned all those nasty words from you. It's your fault, your fault, do you hear me?"

She ran after me with a vigorous spanking in mind. I locked myself into the bathroom, allowing plenty of time for her anger to evaporate before I emerged. That was my only choice because I couldn't run. Escape was always premised on sober forethought and fast reflexes. My poor grandmother often intervened between my mother and I God bless her soul, whatever cloud she is lying on now.

"You are going to kill that poor child, you witch!" she snapped to my mother. "Leave her alone. She didn't do anything. After all, they're just a few nasty words... that's all."

"Don't interfere and mind your own business," responded my mother.

"Stay cool in your corner and don't speak. I brought her into the world and I'll send her to the underworld if I want."

"You ugly cow, where are you going?" I blurted out to my retreating mother.

"Are you leaving us alone again, with your going out all the time? Do you have a boyfriend? I'll tell my dad when he comes home."

My mother looked after everything and everybody; it was a result of my father working irregular shifts in the naval administration. She bore the daily burden of responsibility for us all.

When I turned thirteen and went to high school I carried my first woman's bag. I put a pink dress on, second-hand altered by my mother, and went for a walk. I was going to take the bus for the first time. Back then the buses were third world vehicles that moved very slowly and left black clouds in their wake. Old iron junkers, most of them. My country hadn't yet modernized.

They were very high for the passengers to board and therefore had three big stairs. Me, being short and disabled, it wasn't so easy to climb those stairs. That's why I invented a trick. I let buses pass right on by without boarding just because they hadn't stopped next to the curb upon which I stood. I would wait for the next bus, hoping it would stop next to the curb. Ascending was a bit difficult, but descending was easier. I was wearing my kits brace on my leg that identified me to everybody in the neighborhood, I left my traces in the dirt everywhere and people called me by popular name:

"Ah, you mean that 'cripple girl' who is shopping here? She lives down there on the corner."

That was the code word — "cripple" — to find out about me and my pin number would have been something like my date of birth or my age by that time. Now, it is easier, someone can look at it in Google, then it was different. People readily stared at you, they pointed at you with their fingers and they imitated your walking, your voice and your behavior. Third world country, natives!

As though I didn't have a name. For the entire neighborhood, I was the "cripple."

Who cares now?

But then it was so different.

It broke my heart to hear —instead of my well sounded name— that terrible name that isolated me from everyone else. I was so scared, I didn't want anybody to remind me of my disability. I looked at myself in the mirror and I liked what I saw from the waist up. I never looked at my legs because I didn't like what I saw. It was the period in my life that I didn't like myself at all. I just wanted to die right there in the middle of my virginity and innocence just because of people's stupidity that took the form of laughter and pity. I couldn't stand it anymore. I hated the whole world. I wanted to become indeed a terrorist like the Germans Baader and Meinhof, my idols at that time.

The thought of blowing everybody up in the air!

I asked my father:

"Dad, do you have any mines left from the war?"

"To do *what* with those weapons which spread death?" he asked in astonishment.

"Nothing. I only ask if you have some. Can you make a minefield for me, my dear daddy?" I was begging him with devilish flattery.

"Don't talk nonsense. It took us so long to get rid of those mines and now you want me to make a new one? Are you out of your mind?"

My good father was disarming mines in the Middle East during World War II. He was a naval officer, frequently tempting death. Death apparently reconciled with him, for he was still alive when the war concluded.

How was I going to come through my own private cataclysm?

"You know what?" I told him, as though I wanted to open my heart to him. "I would like to wipe some idiots off the map."

"I understand," he told me while patting my head tenderly.

"Be a bit patient till you grow up and you will see that many things don't matter as much as you originally thought. You have to study to become independent, my sweet daughter. To be fully educated, so that everybody will drop to their knees before you and wash their hands prior to touching you. I'm sure you are going to climb high in an unfair world because you are talented and beautiful — but unlucky."

That last word he whispered softly as though I would not hear it.

I heard him indeed and I knew exactly why I was so unlucky. I became invalid and cripple and different from the other people, the natives — to be set apart from the masses, pointed at and the reason people are compelled by our superstitious religion to make the sign of the cross when I passed.

"God save us, god save us from the infection," they said while they spat three times on the earth while turning their heads on the right side to cast the devil out.

"Is that contagious?" they asked my mother.

I was the infamous "infection," compelling some mothers to avoid me so as to preclude the same fate for their children. Like in Spinalonga, a Greek island, where in past times, lepers were exiled for the supposed benefit of the healthy.

That was my 'wonderland' where I grew up that time. Cinema called the paradise and I was shooting a film, I was the super star, the leading actress! My life was undoubtedly spectacular!

Every night I made my bed, I slept in the living room and my brother with Babis slept in the other bedroom. I had the hope of waking up from a bad dream, a nightmare. If I survived from the bad thoughts, I intended to commit suicide one day. I wanted to commit suicide but I was so scared even to think about it. I was such a coward, a chicken. The thought of it caused me to shudder from head to toe. Unfortunately, I wasn't brave enough to take that risk so I had to put up with the consequences of my hesitation to put an end to my life; that being more and more suffering at the hands of the 'native people'. How could I escape from the people who swore at me, relegated me to an outcast, and pitied me unbearably?

"Look at that poor child, how is she walking? Why has God punished her?" they asked each other staring surprisingly at me.

"Parents' sins follow their children!" I loudly responded, compelling them even more so to keep staring at me with curiosity.

"God save me!" I would shout.

"Mother?" I asked one day.

"Could you please tell me if you ever had an incestuous relationship that has resulted in my becoming like I am?"

"A crazy priest has surely christened you," she said.

"Indeed, he was crazy. But it was your choice, not mine," I said.

"You were so healthy and beautifully born, like a small lobster. But then when we went to Constantinople you became seriously ill. Do you have to blame me for that, too?" she stated as tears formed in her eyes.

At the time I must have been very cruel because in defense of myself, I didn't care at all. "I didn't say it was your fault, I just asked a question. That's all."

After a while, pretending I didn't see her tears, I asked again.

"And why did we have to go to Constantinople?"

"To visit Pelagia, your father's sister. But the blockhead Turkish doctors couldn't find out what it was." She gathered herself.

"Ok, leave it now. I don't want to discuss it anymore. Let bygones be bygones!"

"Not at all bygones," I persisted. "I want to forget and they don't let me."

"Who, which...?" she asked.

"Leave it be. It doesn't make any sense," I answered stiffly.

I was overjoyed and proud to take my first ride in the bus that day in my pink dress. I felt like a young cute lady for the first time, perhaps. I chose the third bus to get on since it fulfilled the necessary requirements. I got on. I validated my ticket and remained standing, supporting myself on the railing since the bus was full and there was no seat empty. Some men offered me their seats. Being ashamed of my situation, I blushed and refused. I didn't want to be different. I said thank you and kept standing, leaning next to the window.

I wanted to overcome the limit of my endurance and I managed very well. They kept on staring at me surprisingly. Counting the stations to get off the bus, I tried to ignore them. I pressed the button for the station and proceeded to the door. Finally the bus stopped. I began to descend on the steps but on the second step I fell to the pavement. My beautiful purse hooked onto a lady walking on the pavement, who came back to help me. My pink dress was blackened with dirt. The worst of all however was that the bus stopped and the driver himself got off to check on me. I wished a hole would open right next to me and swallow me up. A big hole opened on my head instead and it was bleeding compelling passersby to hail a taxi that might take me to the hospital. I refused, they insisted persistently even forcing me to get into that terrible cab.

"Leave me alone," I told them kindly at first. "I am fine, I am not going to the hospital. My house is nearby."

They couldn't understand.

I felt like I was being suffocated by their affection.

"Get out of my way, leave me alone, do you hear me?" I was shouting now and crying at the same time. "I can take care of myself. Get out of here!"

I was probably screaming or howling because all of a sudden they got into the bus and disappeared. With the exception of the lady that my purse had hooked on when I had fallen, I was finally left alone, relieved on the pavement but distressed. My first attempt to know the world had led to disaster. I picked up my purse that the lady returned to me, I thanked her and walked all the way back home.

I lied on my bed and cried. My sorrow had overcome my endurance and reached my grand-mother's ears. Babis, her nickname, was my brother's goddaughter. We were only the two of us at home.

"What has happened to you, my child?" she asked me tenderly.

"Nothing" I said and wiped my eyes.

"Are you hurt or something?" she asked me with concern. "Has anybody hurt you?"

I couldn't resist narrating the whole incident because she saw my head bleeding. She briskly attended to it, fast and good like a nurse and a mother who had raised six children. She looked at me compassionately, not uttering a word. Babis had a very special way to communicate with people. Her silence!

It didn't take me long to forget the whole incident and considered it a challenge to be overcome the next time I would have to ride the bus. I was successful. Nevertheless, I keep on falling sometimes but I stand up again. I jerk my wings like hens do and proceed forth with my waddling gait. Maybe I am a hen —a Paralympics hen, let's say, with special abilities, commonly known as a handicap. Now I'm grown up, and civilized people themselves have transformed into dirty mouth adults that call me.

"Get lost, you cripple chick! Leave us alone!"

But who cares anymore? Now I am the featured hero in a story with power over their lives. I have become so transparent going through all those dirty canals that nothing touches me anymore. I have overcome the most difficult effrontery to contentment — my own body. I jumped out of my original body and have donned a new one that looks almost the same.

Only my eyes I've decided to change. I now look at myself and others with different eyes and I feel great!

The eyes of an owl and not of the hare...!

IRON MAIDEN

The acronym trumpets! Millions of suffering mothers and millions of suffering children. Young and old.

H.U.F.H.C. stands for Hellenic Union for Handicapped Children.

The biggest school of my life! Cinema referred to it simultaneously as paradise and purgatory! Souls in hell! My greatest shame! My only outlet!

My involuntary integration to the Union!

"We are all the same," we are shouting, trying to persuade the 'normal kids!'

"Together we will fight!"

"United we'll claim our rights!"

"Come on, all together, wheel chairs, artificial legs and arms, and all of you handicapped children all over the world, join together in our struggle against all the "healthy ones." Ready ourselves for the Paralympics, without rewards, without prizes, without cheering and applause, just because we are unable to get on the stage of victory to take our prizes. Nobody can do that. Anyway, who amongst us youngsters could raise a wheelchair overhead in triumph?

"Let's bring all the taboos, the lobbies, ghettos down, to get right into their nose, either way, without wishes or curses, so that we'll establish the title we were given. PEOPLE WITH SPECIAL NEEDS. The penance will follow soon enough and the tranquility of our souls will come shortly after just because recognition and fulfillment originate in our souls, but they still have a long way to go before they make their appearance. We all thought that our sortie from that inferno would make our life easier. How easily we were deceived!"

Purgatory and Paradise were expecting us there on their respective thresholds right just when arrived, shouting happily in relief, "At last!" The executioners were expecting us. They were tracking every difficult step we made so as to terminate us without mercy, without compassion, without shame. Helpless, completely helpless we went up the new stairs of our independence. Most of us gave up without resistance, the rest survived hauling up their past lives in tow, the experiences behind them now converted into inferiority complexes. Some others proceeded further and their experiences were turned into the personal center piece of a melodramatic sport between their fellow initiates to the H.U.H.F.C. The last ones were the real winners.

As for myself, I survived being thrown of Keadas[2] cliff because I am very flexible like a snake and my body oscillated madly in the air before hitting the bottom. It was a tremendous fall but I survived. I didn't even have the time to make a confession in front of the priest before they had brought me face to face with death. I've never thought I would have

---

[2] A cliff on Taygetos mountain from which in ancient Sparta all disabled and deformed children were thrown down

been discarded like garbage. So I jumped out of my crippled body and became physically strong. Having survived the crash, that's why I am able now to now narrate my comedy. Yes, it's about a comedy. My life is a big comedy. Somebody played a hoax on me. That's the way I feel about it —a farce with the objective to make fun of me and submit my ailing backside to strong restorative injections. My buttocks have been pierced from so many injections that I'm thinking of buying new ones. Do you know where they sell things like that?

There in that institution I've spent my childhood with the weak hope in my arms. Those like me were far from the conventional implements of society's cruelty, the guns and the weapons. Later in life this separation would end, but during those tender years we lived inside a ghetto which protected us along with our families. We were never left alone in the H.U.H.F.C. But that ended with graduation.

The school bus was coming to take me to school. White like an ambulance it was, and on its side a terrible sign with red thick letters was written: Hellenic Union for Handicapped Children. I was so ashamed to be taken to school in such a terrible bus that was little more than a rolling stigma. Before boarding I would have much preferred that the earth tear asunder and consume me right then and there.

While in the bus everything was tolerable. At times I even felt like I was going to a fantastic private Greek school, because at that time only the rich people's children attended schools with transportation specifically dedicated to their needs.

How could they have those terrible buses with those terrible letters? Why should everybody know who we were? I felt so heavily stricken by that terrible disease, called poliomyelitis, something I wanted so earnestly to forget.

I wanted to look like the rest of the children. I didn't want to be an exemption to the rule. I didn't want to live in a ghetto. Stop!

In that cursed inferno, the real center of handicapped kids, or "Special Needs People," the main sponsor was the king from the Kaiser's family, led by the terrible Rasputin Queen Frederick in concert with many benevolent families which visited us from time to time. We bowed deeply in front of her and kissed her hand. Scorn for the powers that began later on with our political awaking. We had been so effectively brainwashed we could not act other than what was prescribed by others unless we made a great gash in our heads to upload new data so as to correct the involuntary lobotomy we had already been subjected to. That would be a long and painful procedure.

The benevolent Queen visited us quite often, particularly during celebrations and parades with her daughters, Sophia and Irene. I still keep the photos of the events at school where we gave gymnastic exhibitions of the physical abilities that we could demonstrate.

It must have been during the last year of primary school when one pupil was appointed to offer a bouquet to the Queen. That student was me. I was the lucky and honored one to have that task because I had the best grades in the class. With my heart beating loudly and gaily in light of the prestigious honor afforded me, in my blue shorts and my short-sleeved t-shirt with the label of the Union pinned on the left side, with my well-fitted and sophisticated brace on my leg and my cumbersome gait, I walked through the immense body of onlookers comprised of the 'healthy ones'. I crossed the threshold to reach the front seats where the Queen was sitting together with her daughters, the archbishop, and the rest of the aristocratic attendees. I was careful to walk with great awareness not to stumble, not to fall, not to become the ridicule of the school in front of the multitudes waiting just for such a spectacle to add perverse interest to the solemn event.

I gave the bouquet to the Queen and kissed her hand before kissing the hands of her coterie to her left and right. The last kiss was that of the Arch bishop. I felt like biting his hand but I didn't do it. Since time immemorial I had had a terrible allergy and disgust for the apostles of the church, dressed up in canonical garb that most likely concealed their own personal defects. A distinct probability. Generally speaking, I did not like masks of any form. I needed to have clear things in front of me. That's why I don't like the sequestered beauty and cloistered vanity implicit in the garments of women almost everywhere in the Middle East.

So I kissed the hands of all the VIPs that were visiting our school and then I made a spectacular turn and started my way back, with my soul and hands free in front of that terrible crowd, as if my clumsy gait was synchronized to the ceremonial anthem that the band played. Limping mostly on the left side, I lurched like a small fishing boat, not being used yet to the blowing of the wind and the wild storm of the sea, right into that terrible heat of June, perspiring and puffing all the time. There was no pride —only shame— at being used as an exotic servant to the king's family. Once more I felt like drowning myself.

I hated all the "healthy ones" of society, but most of all the small kids and the old ladies. The kids staring at you with those persistent, innocent eyes that was followed by the routine asking of silly questions, and the purposely hurtful inquiries by the elderly which were humored by the behavioral liberties afforded the victims of Alzheimer's Syndrome.

When I detected the enemy with my antennae, I immediately put on my helmet and my ear protectors so that I would not hear what they had to say before running as fast as my lame leg allowed. I hid under shelters, shutters, doors, yards, corners, anywhere possible. Torture! If somebody was persistent in seeking me out, it would be a particularly bad and unfortunate day. The mockery, excoriation, and wonderment underlined the persistent reality that — to the healthy ones— no river could wash away my sins.

"Just look at her, the way she is walking, like a sinking boat," said one.

"No, she looks like a lame duck, ha, ha," said another.

"What has happened to your leg? Eh, do you hear? We are talking to you. Don't pretend you don't hear!"

"You cripple, cripple, wait, wait. Don't go! We won't harm you! Just wait!"

As a sharp knife the words thrust into my flesh at that time in my life, but later on I learned to repay them with contempt of my own; to swear at them and enthusiastically familiarize them accordingly with their own all-too-apparent defects. It was only then that when in fear of being insulted themselves did they start to respect me. Street justice.

"Why don't you look at yourself? You blind devil, blind devil!" I said to one onlooker wearing glasses.

"Get out of my way you fat ugly pig, you are calling me cripple, have you ever seen yourself in the mirror?" I said to another.

"Look at your face with all those freckles. Look at it! What has happened to you? Somebody has probably punched your nose or has it looked so flat since your birth?" I repeated without mercy and sympathy.

This is how I learned to survive in that society of the small heroes. In a society of cowards incited by the petty opportunism that a disable person provides.

We, the imperfect associates of the H.U.H.F.C., started fighting and playing with our defects and weaknesses, to speak them out without fear and shame. And if some stranger dared to encroach upon our dignity with mockery, we returned his aggression. Being effective meant that we learned to measure and sharpen our words before delivering them on target. Discretion was, indeed, often the better part of valor, for otherwise our mutual inner turbulence would have drowned each of us in the enormity of our collective acrimony.

There in the middle of the road behind the barracks a battle was taking place. There I took my first lessons of self-defense. For me it was a battle of survival. I had to survive any way that I could, legally or illegally, and gain respect and admiration; otherwise I would have been lost into my mother's arms and my father's secure palms. In the grimy streets of Athens where I grew up with the rest of the kids, I had to fight my own battles with both younger and older adversaries. We were the tramps of the neighborhood and we spent very little time at home. My brother was my security guard, ensuring that nobody dared — even as a joke — to say something insulting to me. If so, they would receive a punch in the nose courtesy of my brother.

I've always been a good pupil with the best marks but while I was a scholarly success, at times I was often a behavioral misfortune for the school authorities and my schoolmates. A real patron of mischief! That's the origin of my name, too — Zavolia— meaning mischief, a rascal, somebody who is disobedient and annoys or teases everybody, who causes trouble all the time and escapes punishment. A small dot moving dangerously around, turning everything upside down without bearing the consequences of her misdeeds; the latter being a skill that took a long time to perfect.

There were some small incidents concerning my behavior in the H.U.H.F.C. for which I was almost permanently expelled. My mother almost collapse upon hearing of the very misdeeds in which I took so much pride. These incidents raised me to the status of class heroine, resulting in closer scrutiny of me by my brother in fear that the next time I would be expelled.

I didn't care at all for what others thought. I didn't give a damn.

When my mother returned home, she was furious.

"Wherever I go, I feel ashamed of you," she said, angrily pointing at me. Her ire was humorous to me.

"What would have happened if they had to cut his fingers? You have stuck his fingers in the door! My God!" she kept on howling.

"They would have found some new fingers for that poor guy it was an accident. I didn't do it on purpose," I answered. "Anyway, digit transplantation has progressed substantially in the last few years."

"You are completely insane."

"Do you mean 'sensitive'?" I asked her.

"They've warned me you are going to be expelled from school forever."

"The institution, you mean? Thank God, because then I'll go to a normal school with normal children."

"And where are you going to be well treated with physiotherapy and gymnastics?"

"I don't need anything anymore. I'm fine. I was tortured enough, not anymore."

"You must not be well," she said.

"I took it from you."

"You have no respect at all."

"No, it's just that there is little to spare."

"You are rude and insulting and that's why you are going to have a lot of trouble in your life."

"But I am full of courage, aren't I?"

"You don't realize your situation."

"Which situation? I don't understand what you mean."

"I'll tell everything to your father as soon as he comes home."

"Tell him everything. I don't care at all because he is the only one who loves me in this house and you have a negative influence on him."

Then all of a sudden she started screaming and shouting at me and I went and locked myself in the bathroom enjoying my grudges for an extended period of time till she started banging on the door for me to open it.

"Your grandmother wants to go inside. She can't hold herself. Open up!"

Recognizing my grandmother's problem, I opened the door and proceeded directly to the living room where I shut the door behind me. The door to this room had no key. My mother opened that door too and kept on shouting at me. Once she had started her grumbling there was no stopping it until it had run its course much later. God, I wanted to run away from home since I was twelve. My parents loved me in their own oppressive way that was accented consistently with grumbling and shouting. When my mother wasn't grumbling, she was singing. She had a nice voice and a laughter that was pleasant to the ear. To her great credit, she often laughed spontaneously while cleaning the house.

I was so happy when I graduated from that terrible school, I would no longer have to ride in that glorified ambulance for the daily review of all. I was so happy to have abandoned the inferno, the Institution, the reform school. I felt like Oliver Twist and David Copperfield at the same time. A new life was starting for me. My parents thought it was a good idea for me to go to a private school just because the public school was far away from home. They couldn't otherwise afford it but they had managed to set aside some money especially for my education. My high performance on the new school's entry exams was rewarded with a substantial discount on tuition and fees. In addition, the owner of the school was a benevolent man who was well-disposed to those like me who could not walk to the public school.

"Iron Maiden Gymnasium, N.N. Makris."

Only girls attended that school, and they overwhelmingly came from rich families. I had a fantastic time in that school. Alice in the Wonderland, I have been. However, I again felt shame — not because of my limping — but because of my family's lack of wealth. I was ashamed of our house, of my clothes, of the fact that we didn't have a car and so on. Although I had a fantastic relation with all the girls, I had an inferiority complex. They loved me and accepted me the way I was. They fancied my rebellious behavior and I became their leader. I was the first Zavolia in the class and we played jokes with our teachers. We were continuously teasing them, that's why we were at times spanked or slapped because as a Greek proverb says "slapping derived from heaven." I had super teachers and there I got thoroughly educated. There I've started learning to love the school and the people! I felt very normal, equal to the other students.

Perhaps the only material thing I wasn't ashamed of was, ironically, our school bus. In the previous bus, I had become a tiny dot so that no one would take notice of me. But now I was gratified to go to private school in our new yellow bus. It proudly announced to our neighbors that I was attending a private school, as though I had spontaneously transformed myself into a member of the upper class.

But every time my mother went to the school to get my grades she came home gloomy and yellow like a lemon.

"What's the matter, mum? Why are you so blue?" I' asked her eagerly. "Didn't I have good grades? Aren't I going to pass the class? What? What? Tell me!"

"Highly graded but lowly standing," she said with clear disappointment.

"What do you mean? I don't understand!" I asked her again, although I knew precisely to what she was referring: My behavior in class!

"Very good student they said. But they come out of their clothes because of your bad behavior."

"Wow! You mean they take off their clothes when they see me? Am I so sexy, you mean?"

"Why don't you shut your nasty mouth up? The only thing you care about is that...! Why don't you take a look at yourself?! And you think you can make a fuss in class and torture your poor teachers? They'll kick you out of the school and then you'll be barred from every other school in Athens. You'll be relegated to Embirikio School then. There isn't another choice!" She was determined and angry. At that point I began to worry.

Embirikio was a reforming and boarding school for outlaw maidens; its students were comprised of the sinful or the underground, predominantly the lower class, the offspring of families with thousands of problems. The school was located next to our house, and every time I passed by I heard them howling and addressing the passersby with nasty words.

That's why I was shaking all over when I heard that name.

"There? What do you mean?" I asked my mother, pretending I did not care at all.

"I felt so humiliated when I went to your school today. Shame on you! You have become the clown of the school! What's gonna happen with you, can you tell me?"

"I don't know, mum, I may become a good girl later on..."

"When? When you get old?"

"Ha, ha, I scarcely have emerged from my egg shell and you are talking about my elderly years?" I tried to make a joke so that she might change her mood. No way; she declared that she was determined to commit suicide because of the shame and humiliation. And there was nothing I could do!

Four fascinating years I spent in that school, learning and having perfect relations with my schoolmates. They seemed to appreciate me a lot, making me their leader, especially in the frequent playing of jokes on our poor teachers. They invited me to their parties. I grew up in those long parties with fantastic music, soft drinks, dried foods and good-looking young boys who never asked me to dance. This increasingly resonated with me. I don't think they fancied me particularly by that time. That something continued to be wrong with me was apparent. For this I needed remedy because although I was accepted and admired by my friends but not accepted in the male society. This is how I felt — maybe it was simply a product of having low self-esteem. I developed an inferiority complex. I felt too "little" — a small dot again, without a serious reason to live. I admired most of my school mates. They had something special, a free behavior, a cosmopolitan liberty, a flair, modernly dressed. They looked like movie stars to me.

When I was invited to a party, I hesitated to go just because I knew that no one would dance with me. However I did go, ever in search of that integration in the social life of my peers. I allowed fantasy to be my accompaniment — a companion that procured as many dancing partners as I might like.

"If I were Vicky — that good looking girl with the nice body, beautiful long hair, and trendy clothes— wouldn't the boys have liked me? Wouldn't they have asked me to dance?"

I thought so but it wasn't like that. I became a Vicky out of a miracle and I had a fantastic time. Whatever I couldn't reach in reality I reached it through unreality, my imagination. I've been fantasizing and I dared everything and then I felt relaxed and happy.

A kind of meditation, as they call it today.

Then I woke up and I hated myself, urging me to "take a trip" again and again.

They used to call me absent-minded and peculiar, heady, but I cared less and less since I had been traveling all over. When I was weary, feeling lonely, when tears came up in my eyes, I found a good-looking young man to dry them on... and be by my side forever. The only thing I had to do was to switch on the button and I was gone! Most of the times, gone, far away!

All the young ladies in the school were looking for boyfriends. They were flirting and far too modern for my mother's tastes. She hated all those parties and coffee meetings with the rich girls but she could do nothing to stop it. There was no way to prohibit my frequenting those meetings and parties. I was not obedient at all and my father was my ally, although ultimately her dire influence resulted in his capitulation to her wishes. He was influenced by her but at the end he surrendered. I was a fantastic fairy tale narrator. My imagination invented stories to upgrade my social standing status and avert bad endings. I imagined the most daring stories of all kinds. It brought me such joy. If I wanted money, I had it. If I wanted the best looking boyfriend, I had it. If I wanted to be in Honolulu or America, I was instantly there, with only pushing of a magic button. I never imagined though that most of my ideals and goals would come to pass someday. No way! My hopes in those days were so tender and weak! That's why!

During a party I met two sisters who lived with their mother near my house. Their father was a doctor and had passed away in his mid-forties some years ago. They were twins — Eva and Angelika. They invited me to their house and I was so happy to discover both a rich library there and many good-looking boys frequently visiting their house. They organized spiritual gatherings and funny parties. Doing such things was a taboo then but their mother was free-spirited, not at all conservative, nor was she highly educated. I liked their house a lot from the very first time I stepped foot in it; it looked modern and cozy. But the house did not strike my mother the same way. She had a bad word for everybody.

"That's the house of the orgies. You aren't going there again."

I paid no attention to her orders. Nobody was permitted to obstruct my intense desires of that time. I was a young girl after all! I increased my visits to their house because I felt great there — just to see them, to have a small chat, to see a young boy I liked. It became my shelter for those boring Sunday afternoons. I started borrowing their books, thousands of books. There I discovered Kazantzakis, Tomas Mann, Oscar Wilde, Shakespeare, Elitis, Seferis, Eliot, all and everything. I took heavy doses of literature, philosophy, poetry and politics. I read like a maniac. The father of Eva and Angelika was an activist and well positioned in the *Communist Party*. I slowly ventured into prohibited knowledge and prohibited actions which were for my family, only taboos. Besides that, I enjoyed their company and I liked talking with their mother. She wasn't grumbling like mine, and she was very hospitable. They liked my company too and often invited me to take meals and attend their gatherings.

A "gathering" at the twins' house was comprised of some people being together, sharing some good moments, listening to music, dancing, chatting, having fun, having some drinks and playing the "bottle game." It was during the playing of that game that I was kissed by the best looking boy of the gathering — an event that prevented me from sleeping the entire night. To savor the moment I did not brush my teeth so that the taste of that first kiss would not vanish! It was there that I — disabled leg not withstanding — was asked to dance by a boy. A simple act — but a substantial one. In the company of the twins, I started going out to clubs on weekends for the explicit purpose of dancing. *Soul Sisters* became our meeting place.

I urged my father to buy me more books. I soon was receiving monthly installments. The books became my new world. That house came to represent the first station in my journey of creative development in life. However, the social burdens of my disability remained the source of continuous torment. I wanted to change my life for the better. I've been waiting for a miracle, a portentous event, an obliging fairy to change my life with her magic stick, to extricate me out of the misery and acrimony.

I had long had a bitter taste in my mouth with respect to the enduring stigma that my leg represented.

"Why me?"

While I still regularly wore the brace on my leg, I removed it before going to parties or gatherings. I had a terrible inferiority complex that I continuously tried to disregard during such social settings. I took up the guise of the trite optimist that pretended everything was perfectly in order. I wanted to forget my problems but the people everywhere kept on reminding me that I was "different, peculiar, odd, and weird."

"Integration," that is why. I had been desperately seeking to integrate, to relieve my despair with this panacea. I loved people and wanted to be their equal. But my lack of self-esteem created illusions I could not avoid. The children of the 'healthy ones' would become so curious and inquisitive with me at times, staring and glaring as though I was the "monster." Indulged by their mothers, the children were central in making me feel like the "monster." I never wanted to become a teacher but life led me down that path as one way to overcome my inferiority complex with respect to the younger members of society that were so central to implanting that mentality in me.

My long-desired integration though was late in coming, no doubt a sentiment that was a product of impatience. As the years passed there had been improvement in my thinking and appearance, but that still wasn't enough. My integration followed a painful acknowledgement of another affliction that plagued me a peculiar disposition to "bear the sins of the whole world…"

My fate!

BICYCLE, OH, MY LOVE, AND THEN…
THE U.S.

Love met me on my red and black speedy bicycle in a small coastal and picturesque village, Agios Theodoros, a few kilometers far from Athens, almost tipping me over in the process. I remain deeply attached to those raw and rare years! A Mauritian prince on his white horse, his bicycle!

My immediate family used to have holidays there with Aunt Sophia and her two boys. Our fathers visited us on weekends and we spent some good times together. We, the younger ones, befriended same-aged locals and holidaymakers, swimming at the beautiful beaches during daytime, and at nights eating souvlaki, going to cafeterias, on occasion dancing at outdoor clubs.

I met Georgis on the beach. He came from that village and he was very good looking. He did not belong to our group but I had picked him out of all the boys in our small 'company' because he had a gorgeous body and a handsome face, very manly. He looked like a foreigner and he spoke without that annoying terrible accent of the locals. He was refined and stylish, modern in dress, not boring and he had the best smile in the world. He looked more or less like Harry Belafonte, the famous Black Caribbean singer of that time. On top of that, he had the trendiest bicycle in the whole village. He always rode his bicycle as though he was explicitly looking for something or somebody. We met many times with our bicycles, often exchanging hot-eyed peeps. Two summers like that passed by, meeting while riding and flirting, sometimes exchanging a shy smile. In the meantime we built our own small holiday house in the village next to my aunt's house. Sadly but not fearfully, nothing happened with Georgis. Once I thought he had been following me, but that was apparently a figment of my imagination.

That was all.

So, I fell in love with him. I was so crazy about him, being the subject of many of my dreams. It was joyous. However platonic, it was a fantastic relationship!

That year, my parents decided to send me to America — specifically to my Aunt Irene and niece Lizeta to see some doctors about my leg. America was very advanced in the medical sciences. A cousin of mine suggested that I should stay there for a year, attend an American school, and find out more about the continent that Columbus discovered. When they asked me if I was interested, I agreed immediately. Why shouldn't I? A new world was opening for me! I left half of my heart with my family and friends and the other half with Georgis and I headed for the New World, like poor women who went to America as pre-selected brides for unknown men whom they had seen only in photos, immigrants, looking for wives to start a family.

Thousands of new impressions and experiences promptly made me forget everything about my poor country.

My new country surprised me tremendously! Above all, the people! I got crazy about the people — open-hearted, easy-going and friendly with a pinned smile on their mouth and a compliment for all. Very communicative, they touched me and took me in their arms, they kissed me, paying me always more compliments. They seemed to like everything about me. Unlike back home, in their eyes I was not in effect a UFO anymore — just a normal young girl with some difficulties she could overcome.

That was it! I felt like a princess, like a star, and that was a very reconstructive injection indeed. Maybe the first pleasant injection of my life. A narcotic of sorts without any addictive after effects with respect to love and affection. You missed it but you needed it not. I started forgetting my handicap. I felt equal and not different, not peculiar at all. It was the first time I found out about my individuality, about myself. My turbulence relented. I let things go. I improved my appearance just because my inner self had been improved, and for the first time in my life I felt I looked somewhat beautiful and young like other young people. Part of their group, and not "apart" from their group!

My cousin and her two sons also did their best to convey my worth. One son was two years older than me and the other was four years older. "Smart and talented," they called me, and I did my best to live up to their assessment. I felt intuitive and creative. I was transformed from the tiny dot into a big strong bullet with mass, gravity and power. People made me happy instead of gloomy and desperate. A mixed social group of people were everywhere to be seen — white, black and yellow, dark blue and dark yellow, very white with freckles and red hair, fat and thin, handicapped and healthy. All mixed together, caring about their own lives and not about the others. Under normal circumstances such differences were translated into a constant struggle for privilege and survival. That was my first quick impression of America. The country became my combined shrink, psychoanalyst and remedy. Even when I visited some ghettos of Negroes where my Aunt Irene had some friends in Garrison, Maryland, I was never looked down and humiliated as in my own country. Even the kids were looking at me as a normal person and not with such annoying curiosity. They approached me because I was Greek and they touched my hands, my hair. They looked at me straight in the eyes. The old ladies in the inner city ghettos smiled at me, implying:

"So what, go ahead, you look fine."

America, America became my earthly paradise, my shelter, my nest of constant creativity and wonder. There I started slowly rising and shining as I had so rarely done in the past, and I seemed to take some of their faded sunlight. I was suddenly illuminated, blinded by the intense light. So much light I've never seen before. I procured it and made it mine, bringing it back with me to Greece. Individual light, my own light — enlightened!

America, America, the first big station of my life but not the last…

East High School, Denver Colorado. The public school I attended for a year. Students of all races and colors, of all kinds of forms and grounds. A new world for me. However I never felt out of the crowd. I never felt I was something odd, strange. I never felt I was "crippled." On the contrary, I was totally integrated with the world around me for the first time, I became a part of their body. Their attitude emotionally stood my bent form upright and straight. I felt like a queen in that world of admixture and possibility.

At first they placed me into a "welcome class" that was comprised of foreign students where we attended intensive language courses. The first step towards our integration. The remainder of my classes were taken with the American students. The school itself supported our fast and smooth integration into the American reality. There was a special ceremony organized especially for the foreign students in the school's big assembly room where we introduced ourselves to the rest of the students in a ten-minute speech, in English that was terrible at that time. A wonderful experience. Seated on a stage, were made up a panel of about fifteen students, originating from China, Cuba, Spain, Italy, Greece, Thailand, India and Africa. Gosh, like a conference! Microphones, plants, photos, and we well-dressed and neat, embarrassed a bit in front of a crowd of thousand students and teachers. There was clapping and applause, and at the end, the audience asked questions. What an experience for me coming from the country of my birth!

"What brought you to our country?" one of the students asked me.

I was very flexible in answering that question; I did not want to refer to the special reasons that brought me to their country, that's why I invented the word...

"Multi-culture!"

Clapping and applause.

"What do you fancy most in this country?"

"Your modern and progressive society adjusts to the needs of the present. It's the Treasure Island of my dreams!"

Clapping and applause.

At that time American was boiling over with, LSD, heroin and racial strife. However I left aside any mention of that negative side. My real concern was I, myself, my quick integration into the society of the "healthy ones."

I learned that lesson well in America.

"What don't you like?"

"I like everything!"

Laughter.

"Why in Denver and not in California, let's say?"

"My relatives are here and I am a guest at their house."

"Do you think that our educational system is different from the one in your country?"

"Completely different."

"To the best or the worst, according to your opinion?"

"To the best. I find it very convenient and profitable, it helps the students a lot to express themselves freely and thus learn more and faster."

Clapping and applause.

"How does this mixed-colored school appeal to you?"

"For me, it's an awesome experience since we still don't have students from other countries. It's only us, Greek students."

"Are you against or for that kind of school?"

"Definitely for, because we all have to learn a lot from other cultures and civilizations. I said in the beginning, that multi-cultured society attracted my attention. It's fascinating!"

Long simmer clapping and applause.

I noticed that the Negroes were clapping and singing like everyone else, but some of the teachers ordered them to be quiet.

"Mixed school" was then a school for blacks and whites, for colored people, as they were kindly called and not "Negroes." Only as an insult or an expression of casual contempt were they referred to as "niggers." On the surface, the U.S. was more tolerant than us Greeks with respect to the integration of racial and ethnic differences, but it was largely superficial, underneath the multicultural society there was a pool of boiling antipathy, like a volcano preparing to erupt. The racial problem seemed to limp along like me, apparently ambling forth without remedy from what I've seen later on.

Racism in America, discrimination in Greece. The skin color in America, the form of your body in Greece!

Are finally all the countries the same?

When we got off the panel, there was another formality of good will. Some of the students of the "welcome country" came to shake our hands, to touch us, to put their arms around us or even kiss us in both cheeks, flattering us about our "bad English" and the interesting speeches we had just given. Since that day, we were greeted everywhere we met at school, we were addressed to, invited to their companies, made place for us in the dining room. We became a part of their small community.

The American people! Its human substance!

"How come you speak English so fluently? Where did you learn it?"

"In a private institution in Greece, called 'frontistirio'!"

"Not at school?"

"Yes and no!"

"What kind of school is that?" they curiously asked. They probably thought that a UFO had come from Greece to speak about "frontistirio."

"Well, it's a kind of a private primary or secondary school, let's say, where students in order to learn have to pay. Their education becomes very expensive."

"But is it effective?"

"It depends on the students and the teachers."

"Is it a kind of a special school which educates students out of school, right?"

"Yes, that's right."

"Who pays the fees?"

"The parents, of course."

"Gosh, incredible! Aren't there any foreign languages taught in the public schools?"

"Of course, but nobody learns that much in those schools because classes do not meet very often, maybe twice a week."

"Jesus!"

They kept on looking with embarrassment and surprisingly smiling at me. What I was saying was something beyond their experience.

Some of the girls paid me nice compliments.

"Gee, you have fantastic hair, thick and shiny."

"And beautiful eyes," a young boy said.

I blushed. I was not used to that kind of flattery.

"What a beautiful country you live in! I've read and heard so much about Greece. I would like so much to visit it!"

Then a good-looking guy approached me with two other black guys.

"Are you a political refugee?"

This was the era of the military Junta in Greece —"The Regime of the Colonels" — that had taken over the country in a coup. Everybody wanted to know what was going on there.

"Have you asked for a political asylum in America?"

"Not at all."

"Tell us a bit about it." They were practically begging to get information about the military Junta in Greece.

"I don't want to talk about politics. First, that's not my main concern or the reason I came here, and secondly I don't have much to say."

"How come? You don't care about politics? That's the A and Z of our life."

"It's not what you think. Try to understand, please!" I tried to get away from that circle.

"Leave her alone, m—an, leave her alone. Can't you see, she doesn't want to talk about it! She might have her reasons. Leave her alone, m—an!"

I was relieved as he pulled the other away, leaving me in peace. I was not particularly affected by the political situation then in Greece. Not because I didn't care but because my attention was principally drawn to my individual problem, and I was convinced that no policy of the political bandits who had seized power could solve it. On the contrary, as I found out later, the particular trajectory of the Junta's political ambitions would soon deprive me of my human rights, used only as a metaphor... "Together with the communists chased like criminals by the military government."

"Aren't you allowed to talk about politics?" another guy suddenly asked me, appearing in front of me as if from nowhere.

"Not at all! I only said I don't want to talk about politics 'cause I don't want to mix politics and pleasure in your beautiful country. Honestly, I don't want to go back!"

The conversation ended there.

I got some very therapeutic "injections" there which I called "self-confidence injections." That was part of my medical treatment in the USA. The doctors claimed that there was no necessity for an operation, recommending that I no longer use the brace on my leg. It could be replaced with a pair of laced shoes with a heel that was higher on the left side so as to support my leg. This was to be augmented with a lot of gymnastics and a lot of swimming in the beautiful sea that is so particular to my country. So I was set free from my terrible emblem, symbol, or whatsoever they call it, handicap. In fact, I limped on the left side a lot, but now it was different. I did not have to carry my mechanical "Cross of the Martyr" — my crucifixion symbol!

America, America, the land of miracles!

I was only sixteen then. I couldn't yet see beyond the limits...

Together with her boys, friends and acquaintances, my cousin and company were great assistants to my integration in America. She took me to the best doctors, the best hospitals, the best schools. She bought me the best of the best to make me feel at home, like her own child, showing me all the consideration that her own boys received. She treated me with love and care — but sometimes with a touch of cruelty as she had promised my father she would in his name. She did all this even though, at the time, she was dealing with a serious drug problem with her older boy, Ted.

My stay there comprised a series of moments that were amongst the happiest of my life so far. Alice in Wonderland, experimenting with new miracles.

I went to school every day. I was having a good time with my two cousins. There were many people visiting the house, people who were seemingly friends of everybody. Celebrations, birthdays, ceremonies, family gatherings, and then traveling around the country — the Rocky Mountains in Colorado, the Great Canyon where so many western movies were shot, Taos, New Mexico, Arizona, California, Los Angeles, Malibu Beach, Beverly Hills, Washington DC, Maryland, New York — all in the company of my Aunt Irene, at first.

There, I learned to love myself, step by step, the way it was to be. To accept my circumstance — something that was made easier by the fact that I was not routinely reminded by others that I was an invalid or an exotic beast in a miraculous circus show. In America I've been with so many handicapped people moving at ease and enjoying comfort and facilities along the streets on wheel-chairs and walking supporting systems, participating in all forms of social activities. A very effective, social security system without discrimination.

People with "special needs" as we still call them nowadays in my "third-world" country! Why don't they call us Paralympics people and so on?

There it was, I and that "I" I've learned gradually to love and appreciate.

"Self-confidence," "self-esteem," "self-appreciation" injections. At that time, in Greece they were not even being imported!

USA, my first Big School! My best doctor!

Later on I would come to judge that country because of its political interference in everything, the great trusts, the weapons lobbies that seemed to rule the whole world. The longer I lived in the U.S. I got more and exact information as to what was behind its façade, behind my careless and airy youth, behind my cousin's family, and the rest of the other families I've met. America and Greece; my big schools. In America I had been caressed like a pet; in Greece I had been slapped and kicked like a dog, since pets were treated like beasts there. I was one of them!

I had not missed my country for a whole year, neither did I ever turn my head to look back — with the exception of my family which preyed on my mind. However I had to proceed forward and absorb the new. In my free time I was drawing clothes, "modeled," as my cousin called it. She proposed to extend my visa in America so that I might study at the Higher Modeling School because she and her artist friends considered me to have talent. I refused! Probably because I did not have enough self-esteem to believe that I was talented! I could not even dare to think about it. God — I — talented? My physical problem acted like a brake on my personal advancement.

In the U.S. I learned a lot. The lessons were fantastic, but it took me a long time to make those lessons concrete and realize a profit from them all. The self-knowledge procedure took me a long time, and in the interim the process deprived me of all the privileges of this new form of "freedom." The normalization of the inner and outer self has been a time-consuming process. Perhaps if I had stayed longer in America it would have accelerated that process, whereas in Greece it once again became extremely slow and painful. However, by the end of my staying in the U.S. I became homesick. I missed my "third-world" country, its primitive social universe.

I regretted my decision afterwards but it was too late.

I left the New World after a year, one hot and humid day in July from New York sitting on the deck of the transatlantic ship *Anna Maria* gazing at the Empire State Building amidst the skyline of Manhattan, that country of fundamental contra-dictions and universal fundamentals it shared with my own country. A farewell to nice memories, to the new I, perhaps...? In retrospect, the U.S. had been an epiphany for me. And that is certainly truth!

The most fascinating trip EVER!

"Home" is nostalgia. Nostalgia, being a deceptive word!

I needed those deceptions though to come back. My illusions were my yearning to see again what I've left behind. That is to say, a longing for my own people; my family was not an illusion though — rather a fact.

The *Anna Maria* was sailing slowly now. After twelve days she entered the deep blue water of Piraeus harbor. We were welcomed with marching and folklore songs performed by the musical band of the local authorities. I fell into the arms of my people, my father, my mother, my brother and grandma. I cried with them, too. I was under the influence of a great emotion, purified and intoxicated by all kinds of germs and negative power, and suddenly I heard there in the middle of the dock one of the porters reminding me clearly that I was now on Greek soil:

"Hey, why don't you move out of the way to avoid another accident with your other leg, too? *Move, move*, can't you hear me talking to you? You cripple!"

"Please don't sail away, you sailors and captains, you big and proud easily-sailed ship, Anna Maria, wait for me, take me back to America, sail on cruises all over but far away from my country since the water here is dirty with pollution and I can't clearly see the bottom any more...," I ordered secretly with small tiny tears at the side of my eyes. It was too late, though, too late. Unluckily, I was back and there was no way out.

"At least you can float, you small idiot... Come on, hold yourself from the buoy and swim, stay on the surface. Stay there, only there, don't move, don't let yourself sink into the bog and mud..."

GREECE, MY POOR COUNTRY

As soon as I kissed the sacred soil of my country, I started cursing and swearing like a truck driver again. It was not necessary to look at the dictionary for those words to refresh my memory since I had been bombarded the whole time in all quarters of society by thousands of such words and expressions. A whole year had passed in the U.S. where I hadn't had to resort to such expressions, but they remained stored securely away in my subconscious, ready to be deployed as soon as I came into contact the familiar environment that so readily triggered my spitting out those atomic bombs. With the exception of my Aunt Irene, I had not articulated a Greek word the whole time in the U.S. My cousins did not even speak a single Greek word!

The first time somebody in Greece called me "dummy" made me burst into tears. The second time, I became furious, and the third time I paid him back with a similar insult — so fast was my reintegration in my own country.

A pain free homecoming? Absurd!

By the end of the first month I had been totally adjusted to the conventional way of life, living in Athens, where everybody used nasty words to each other, at any time, by mouth or by gesture, and mainly while driving. Hot temperament of the Greeks..!

After long discussions and family gatherings, my parents decided there was no reason for me to continue my studies in a private school, since I could walk much better now and without the brace. I agreed with them since I desired the change as much as they and since they could no longer afford such an expense.

Here I am, at the small old chapel, used as an extra classroom for the needs of the 5th Senior High School in downtown Athens. A school exclusively for girls, as was the convention of the day that mandated gender segregated schools. Thank God, there weren't any electric bells otherwise we would have been hearing them clinging every hour.

Being short, I was seated at the last desk, leaning on the humid wall of that old chapel with Demy, a very tall and good friend of mine who was continuously laughing without reason. She seemingly could not help herself from doing so. That was the reason she was sitting there, to hide that terrible vice that was her laughter, otherwise she would have been dismissed from class. Although I was short, I sat next to her because I liked to make fun and tease everybody. However it was a public school and our headmaster was very strict. Mr. Pelopoulos, a nice looking middle-aged man with grey thick hair, was so severe that all of us were trembling from fear at his sight. For some odd reason he had always been very kind with me, smiling at me and greeting me the whole time. I was wondering if there was probably somebody handicapped in his own family so as to explain his exceptional disposition towards me. I had already started feeling independent, that is, not caring so much about other peoples' opinion. Perhaps he liked my smart face which often seemed to instantly charm my enemies.

However, during those tender teenage years I could never admit I was at all charming or attractive in anyway.

Once more there was a serious event at school concerning my behavior, and that made me not only to like Mr. Pelopoulos but indeed begin to fall in love with him — something I realized was happening when he became the featured person in the wild travels of my imagination. I cheated during graduation exams, an act that resulted in my being brought to his office to receive punishment. He did his best in order to avoid being overly harsh with me since my teacher was asking for "my head on a plate." He succeeded in salvaging my reputation otherwise I would have been, once again, expelled from school. Nevertheless, he could not save the big 'F'(fail) I had on my final marks!

My mother had almost a heart attack when she saw my grades!

"Let it be," I thought, being much influenced by the popular Beatles' song at the time.

That was the last year of my school life. I finally graduated and I was preparing for the exams to enter University in September, involving a lot of studying during that fascinating, seductive summer of my country. Days and nights full of ecstasy, love, passion, fun, enjoyment...

It was then that I met love in the face of Vlastos. A terrible name that did not fall pleasantly on the ear, nor the imagination! I liked him but not his name, and most of the times I called him "pssst," "eh, you," or made a hissing noise with my mouth to attract his attention, like "tsok, tsok, tsok" as though he were a dog or a cat. Given that name, it seemingly left me no other alternatives.

"*Saturday afternoon and acetylene...*" singing now the melody of a Greek song.

A sweet afternoon, at the end of spring and the beginning of summer, in all colors and scents to golden our carefree youth; four good-looking young ladies were sitting, chatting and laughing of course as only the young people can laugh before they lose that smile entering the adulthood, at Flocafé somewhere downtown Athens. Me, amongst them! It was planned later on to go to the movies. It was Demy, my tall classmate, her sister even taller, 1.90 cm, another friend basketball player even taller and among them, I, 1.57 cm. Just think of the image. We standing in array!

I wore a very fancy white dress, narrow and sexy with a deep low neck shape according to the demands of fashion. I had also ironed my curly blond hair and let it wave in the air in concert with the afternoon breeze. I was a bit tanned due to my exposure to the sun. I had forgotten my "abject situation," "my downs," my "terrible life" and I was enjoying my youth!

Suddenly I noticed a well-built, tall, and good-looking young man with dark brown curly hair and white skin in his mid-twenties. A little bit overweight — but attractive. He approached our group, kissing Demy first, her sister, before greeting their friends. But in an instant his eyes fixated on me.

"Come, I want you to meet my friend, Zavolia," my friend Demy said.

He extended his arm, and it was indeed an extension, or so it seemed to me. "Nice meeting you," he said. And looking straight into my eyes, he added, "I've never seen you with the girls here before."

"It simply happens," I said rather indifferently.

I was not particularly impressed. I found him a bit soppy. He stayed with our company for a while, being pleasant and humorous. And then he left. Soon thereafter, Demy invited him to the movies with us but he refused. That's all.

Next morning the telephone rang. It was Demy.

"Vlastos is mad about you. He called me last night and was incessantly asking and talking about you. He admitted to liking you a lot and wants to date you. He asked for your telephone number but I didn't give it to him. I wanted to ask you first."

"Ah, what did he have to say about me?" I asked, as though I didn't care at all.

"'Where did you find that blond Goddess... Gee, I fancy her a lot. I want to go out with her. Give her my telephone number or give me hers. She looks fantastic!' That is what he said. What do you think?"

"I am not so crazy about him but I don't have anything to lose if I just date him once."

I was so flattered having my first real admirer from the male sex. I was still emotionally committed to my platonic — albeit desperate love — in Korinthos, Georgis. I had focused my efforts towards that goal.

Bringing me back to the moment, Demy asked, "What should I do? Shall I give him your phone number?"

"Did you tell him about my 'problem'? The guy saw me seated and thought I was a model."

"Of course, I told him and he said he doesn't care at all. He is crazy about you. Can't you understand that? What are you thinking of? Good looking, young, smart, well-off."

"How old is he?"

"Two years older than us. He graduated from school two years ago and he has been working at his father's business."

"All right, all right, I'm not so eager because I hate his name. Jesus, how should I call him? Vlastos? What an awful name. Ha, ha! If his name was Kostas, Yiannis, Giorgos, I would have liked him better. His name pisses me off a lot. Ppppf! All right then. Give him my phone number!"

Indeed it was the first time a boy was falling in such a conventional and intense fashion for me — for which I was extremely flattered. Finally I had attracted the attention of a man just the way I was. It was the source of great appreciation. Why shouldn't I try my luck in love? This is how my erotic heart beat then, and since I did not have another choice, I surrendered!

He called the next day, very easy-going and communicative, asking me to go out with him for a coffee and a nice chat. We met at a café and soon left to see a movie. In the middle of the film he asked me very simply and spontaneously to become his girlfriend, confessing that he had fallen for me from the first moment we met! Wooow!!! He was clear and direct, hearty and sensitive, traits that seemed native to young people who had not yet been introduced to hypocrisy and elusiveness.

We were those fantastic young people that the cinema often portrayed, and the rambling walks, the café meeting spots, and the dancing parties with the dry foods and soft drinks accentuated our affection. We basked in each other's company and comrade-ship, seeming free of the ever present alienation that had been increasingly encroaching upon those entering adulthood. We were the young people of books and good music, of school and fun, seemingly free of frustration and stress. We were the young ones of the multi-membered family gatherings. With our individual problems. We went through our youth at once easy-going but not at ease. These were difficult times where the boiling political passions of the country were coming to a head, where events and revelations were developing so fast and so unexpected that we scarcely had time to react to one before the next presented itself. We were under the dictatorship of Papadopoulos — a government of military bandits who imposed a strict black-out on all forms of social life and communication. It was justified by the reality that our parents had recently come out of a terrible war, and a period of stability could only emerge amidst the distraction and security that authoritarianism could provide. The supposed problem and the terror of that time was the specter of "communism." The communists were portrayed as the terrorists of our healthy society and became refugees at the end in their own country. Our parents tried their best to keep us children from getting drawn into the dangerous politics that were being played out nation-wide.

At least that happened in my family, because my father was a marine officer and just because he had served during the war in the Middle East and had developed a broader way of thinking. He had understood far earlier than most the dirty game played by some of our "democratic governors" in conspiracy with the foreign Kings and the allies, like our "friends," the British. He knew the political machinations of the times very well. He knew that our present military government was a game in their hands used against the *Communist Party* and the partisans' great success who rose up their resistance against the German battalions on the Greek mountains. These were the traitors, an oligarchy of some wealthy opportunists, ruling and ruining up to date our lives.

The Greek people acted and reacted very enthusiastically and spontaneously with bigotry and passion, and most of them did so just because of a distinct lack of education and illiteracy allowed them to be easily manipulated by any corrupted politician. We became our own executioners. The military government did not just materialize from nowhere in our country. It had been propagated and cultivated during those years by the incompetence and consent of our politicians over many years.

Families, relatives, friends belonging to the political left or right otherwise peaceful idealistic people who have never before seen a gun in their lives, became themselves the persecuting hands and feet of the repressive state. They became the very face of violent hatred. They knocked on the doors of their countrymen, being authorized to search and arrest anybody who they deemed suspicious according to their variable tastes, momentary passions, and irrespective of evidence. In the name of their so-called democracy, they sent innocent people to concentration camps, into the exile, confinement on penal islands. They were tortured in the dark basements of *Special Security Police*, similar to the terrors of the German *SS* who had reigned supreme in Greece within the living memory of most. Deaths mounted at the hands of the state-sanctioned torturers.

We lived with a father belonging to the conservative party because he was a naval officer and we were in a way, let's say and I am ashamed to say that, protected, that is to explain, restricted. We couldn't say much, we couldn't do much. The only thing we had been hearing was:

"Gosh, we've gone through so much torturing and violence by those tramps the communists during the Civil War after the real war with the real enemy, the Germans. I don't want to even relive the memory of it."

My mother said: "Our house was commanded by the communists and all of us lived in one room. Thank God that Kostas and Giorgos were serving in the Middle East during that time otherwise we would have all been killed."

"They have even killed our lovely cat, K.K.E.[3], even though it carried their own name.

The communists were the immediate source of our fear and our terror — the "leftists" they were generally referred to. But they also were the source of our hope for a better future, for me and my brother, for our friends, for our acquaintances, for our secret gatherings. We were constantly attacked by the whole family, uncles, aunts, cousins, grandparents and all brandishing anticommunist theories and ideals. Our house was always full of people, mostly relatives, who discussed and

---

[3] Initials standing for the Communist Party in Greece

quarreled over politics; the most actual subject for discussions; my father supported the right political party *ERE*, and my uncles belonged to the middle conservative party of Georgios Papandreou. The Left Party was forbidden in our families. We were not even allowed to write its name.

"Stay away from those bastards, those thieves, they've ruined our country. The criminals!" howled my father. "Watch your friends and the people you talk to. There are spies everywhere. Nobody knows what tomorrow might bring, perhaps the police to our door."

We were subject to an endless brainwashing, but whom of us really cared? We were already formed and developed, we knew our sympathies, what ideology really appealed to us. We had read a lot about the unknown history of our country, something which our parents and uncles probably lacked. We had been listening to the foreign broadcast stations, *BBC*, *Deutsche Welle*, Greek private stations. We had formed different opinions from the main stream for the regular diet of events that were politicized. We were different kind of people. The rebellion against the Junta of Papadopoulos in the Polytechnic University of Greece stimulated our lives, even till today. We — my brother and I — and our friends had been living under continuous agitation, anxiety and insecurity. We had been transformed by the political facts and events. We were forced to live and think that way and not the way our parents had always wanted us to live. We were our own people, of our own generation, of our own culture and a very different relationship to official history.

Until "Vlastos' era'" I was flying high up in the clouds of my own nirvana and lack of confidence. My individual problem mattered for me and nothing else. That was a luxury for me, to think about politics. My main concern was I — myself. It was very egotistical, very egocentric, I know, but it had been a struggle of survival. Suffering was a dungeon I wanted to escape from. I wanted my shoulders free and light as though I had my wings pinned high upon them. My brother pushed me into political and social thinking during the Junta's reign of power after I had come back from the U.S. These were my first steps into the realm of politics.

Then I was baptized and purified by Georgis, my first and big real love. However, my steps were still very tentative. I invested in little in light of the continuing centrality of my own problem. It plagued me. I was deeply convinced that none of the political pigs in the dictatorship could offer me any relief. I've been living with my nightmares, feeling like I was having a bad dream which only faded upon my awakening. I was longing for a personal sunrise and a new day which never came.

I woke up with a big "why me?" and I went to bed again wondering "why me?"

Once I got into a taxi, the taxi driver started flirting with me.

"You are a very good-looking girl. I would very much like to date you, you see, I've never been in a relation with a 'cripple' and I am very curious about it. What do you think? Do you want to?"

The sharp knife of love stabbed into my back. I really did not know what to say to such a person then.

Now, I know these were his limits.

At times like those I became somewhat short of breath. I could not breathe.

Now, I smile…

I told him to stop the taxi and got off without even paying him.

My deep wish was not to die, on the contrary I was yearning to be alive and enjoy that life. Every night I made my bed in the living room I was wondered whether I would awaken in the morning. At one point I came to realize that the worst nightmares took place while fully conscious and had little to do with being asleep. I had colored dreams I could not paint and majestic flights I could not dare in reality. The occasional flirting boosted my self-confidence, yet it was not enough. The upside-down turn! The transformation of myself that was driven by inner impulses and not from external forces. Time should make its own time and was warning me very strictly pointing at me:

"Don't you ever disturb my own time….!"

The point was that I was not at ease and comfortable with myself. That's why I did not feel well about the common people, my executioners. I felt as though I was standing every moment on the gallows, a vision from the Medieval Era.

Damn it! Exaggerating a bit?

I could not accept me by any means. It was impossible to be in harmony with my divine body. Such an irony… Even after my long stay in America, I was improved, yet not healed… My soul was under heavy pressure. I felt a terrible emptiness deep inside. I was experiencing that very intensively. When each morning upon awaking I saw in front of me a big flashing "Why?" followed by thousands of question marks.

"Spare it, it's only a pet. Kick it out, it's only a pet. Kick it out. Its sick, can't you see? And it's probably contagious," my mother screamed. It was her standard reaction every time I patted a cat or a dog. She once had a dog which died of canine dementia. She had probably her own reasons since she went through all that treatment with big painful injections right into her belly. Then...

Casual abuse was the norm in Greece with respect to the treatment of animals at the time. Thank God, it was no so for people!

To make a long story short, I felt like a poor sick animal which everybody kicked, looked down on and paid little attention, somebody who lived only as an outcast.

"Come up, Zavolia, to read your composition in front of the class," my teacher often said.

That was my only pride and honor held sway at such public moments, not my prejudice and shame. I slowly transformed from a little useless dot I had been to a circle, making circuits around its edge, at last — if but for the e — I was master of my own destiny. Luckily I was not a triangle or even a square or a parallelogram, otherwise I would have bumped into its corners. A circle is something superb on the one hand because you move without obstacles, however it can readily begin to suffocate you if you cannot get out of it soon

Outcast I felt! I was pathetic with a terrible lack of resistance!

'CHEER-UP' INJECTIONS

At last, I had a boyfriend! Vlastos. Blast! What a name!

With Vlastos, I learned the meaning of a normal relationship. We went out almost every day, we went to the movies, to cafeterias, and we walked all around Athens, window-shopping, going to the fairgrounds. He held my hand and kissed right in the middle of the road, and he seemed so at ease when doing so. He was proud to do so, not ashamed. He was huge in physical stature, while I was small. It befuddled me that tall men like Vlastos could be so attached to demure-sized women like me.

We went swimming to Flisvos and Varkiza, very picturesque places not far from Athens. We rode by bus. The deep tan that resulted was the source of no small amount of jealousy from my school mates. It was that time when I increasingly was truant from school and even the preparatory school of frontistirio. My mother, the smart fox, soon became suspicious about my whereabouts.

"Where are you hanging out almost every day? With whom? Why don't you concentrate on your exams? That's the most important thing for you, to get into the university and focus on your studies so that we won't have to bear the weight of your problem any longer than necessary."

"What do you mean? Which problem?"

"Your dowry, I'm referring to. We don't have the money to give your future husband."

"I don't want to give a dowry to any idiot looking for a woman with money."

"Who is going to marry you without a dowry and in your situation? Let's see if your stingy uncle, Scrooge Mac Duck, Mihalakis, would give one of his houses to you!"

"You mean, when the time comes, you'll be repaid too for your services. You are expecting something, too."

My mother used to use bitter, hurting words, not because she was mean but because she wanted to confront my rebelliousness and independence. Her words pierced my heart, but I got over them rather quickly and continued on my chosen course.

Mihalakis was the rich husband of my grandmother's step sister. Who cared about my mother's expensive dreams?

Definitely not me, since I spent a fantastic summer with Vlastos. Wandering and strolling idly about, always ending in cafeterias, swimming, and all the cool things that occur in a healthy relationship between two young people. The only demon in our being together was the frontistirio which I had to attend every morning, to be followed by increasing amounts of study afterwards so as to prepare for the exams in September. Given that we had the whole summer ahead of us, I scarcely concerned myself with excessive attention to my education. I even started playing truant from that small school, not feeling the least bit guilty about it.

On the contrary, prioritizing "love" — the subject of the sacred Goddess Aphrodite — seemingly ennobled my acts of truancy. It was never enough with him just because it was fantastic.

About the consequences — don't ask.

At the end of July my father visited the teachers of that school to ask about my progress. He had his first shock!

He immediately wished to have a personal talk.

"My dear daughter," he said very seriously. "I was informed about your absence from school and I felt so terrible about it. I did not know what to say to the principal. What's happening? Please, tell me and be honest with me."

He was always so sweet with me. He loved me so much — a sentiment I dearly reciprocated. I was his pet love, his beloved daughter. He almost never said no to me. He became a slave to my wishes. What should I tell him? How could I tell him that I was dating somebody and everything else was rendered a secondary concern — if a concern at all?

When I became irritated and angry I spoke rudely to him too, and in plural. I used to address him in plural, polite form. I was swearing in plural, too.

"It's hot sometimes and we go swimming with my classmates. Don't worry, my daddy, I'll study and I'll pass the exams. Please don't worry!"

"You must study more than the rest of your friends. That will be your weapon against life, a way to your independence and personal freedom which will sometimes open the doors of paradise to you. As well as those to hell, but you'll overcome it. Remember my words. I may be dead by that time, but it's your own life, you have to do something about it, to take advantage of your qualities, not let them evaporate into thin air. Independence opens the doors to happiness. Dependence, those to hell. Don't forego your paradise, you deserve it. Well... I'll forgive you for the last time if you promise me you will attend your lessons regularly."

"I promise, dad," I said, before lowering my head, hugging him tenderly, and kissing him on both his cheeks.

I had such a tender and affectionate relationship with my father because he knew how to express his feelings despite being brought up in an orphanage since the age of four, enjoying neither a family's affection nor occasional visits. However he never deprived his children of those expressive feelings that alleviate the hardness in people's hearts. He loved my brother the same way, but he felt forced to distinguish between us because of my handicap. The difficult and unfair path I was to travel mandated that he do so. Whatever I wanted I promptly went to my father for satisfaction. Initially, he said no.

"Why no, dad?"

"Just no."

"But there must be an explanation for that no," I insisted.

"Because NO, that's why."

"There is no meaning in these words, give me one good reason and then I'll understand. Pleeeeeease!"

By the time he got around to presenting a good reason he had already become exhausted by my compliments and begging. His capitulation was at hand.

My mother used to grumble, "You've spoiled her. Don't complain then when..."

That's the reason my brother and I became very affectionate kids. We had piles of feelings inside us to spare and wanted eagerly to share them with other people.

"So, come close to us, to find what is missing in your life; free devotion, love and affection we offer with generosity. Please, come closer, don't push and shove, there are enough goods for everybody. Watch out, you've stepped on my toe."

My mother has always been a considerate, affectionate, and extroverted person, but she taken to so much grumbling that it obscured the ample affections for us that she readily displayed.

At night Vlastos and I used to walk up Lycabettus hill and sit at the small ouzo place next to the big cannon that was fired during national celebrations. Then we walked down the hill and we got lost in the adjoining forest. We sat under the pine trees trying to hear our impassioned hearts. One night, during a very close meeting under the trees, he asked me to make love to him.

I didn't feel like it. I don't know why. It did not fit the moment. So I refused. Maybe I simply wasn't ready for such intimacy yet. I can't explain it — my taboos, who knows. Anyway, it was a disastrous turning point in our love story. Since that momentous night, he stopped calling me. Yes, stopped! He was so selfish, not caring at all about my feelings. He did not even want to discuss it with me. He simply deleted me from his social life. Gone with the wind!

Initially I was very angry and sad, but I realized that it was an impulse for my studying for the exams. So, I madly committed myself to my books as a means of avoiding thinking about Vlastos. It hurt me so much but pondering what future goals was an ointment of sorts for the emotional wounds I was suffering. That was my father's vision and support — something for which I have been eternally grateful for.

"Always go forward," he used to say. "Don't you ever look back — but if you do, do it for the express purpose of fortifying yourself further for the path ahead."

In the middle of August, just before exams, I endured a fierce case of appendicitis. My recovery was not only premised on the removal of an inflamed appendix but in no small measure, it required the removal of much bitterness that had also lodged and festered within me. When the time for exams came, I was not well prepared.

I saw Vlastos again at a friend's party and besides a "hello" he paid no attention to me; it was if I did not exist. He had been dancing the whole time with a young girl that was tall like him. I left the party rather early, unable to bear this final chapter in our story any longer. Secretly I prayed for a place at the university while recalling my father's words: "You have to study and learn more and more and become independent so that you won't 'get stuck' to a problem without being unable to overcome it and continue on."

My father's thoughts were the first step on the way to recovering my self-esteem, meditating deeply on them, and consequently making them watch-words for so many of my life's choices. In other words: *"Push life ahead!"*

Vlastos was pushed clean out of my thoughts in the same fashion, leaving plenty of room for my dreams and targets.

"You fat, ugly guy! You kick 'me' to the curb? I kick 'you' to the curb with nary a second thought. You are so selfish! Besides that, you have a terrible name. I've never fancied it. I've always thought it was a terrible, I just hated it. I think I deserve something better than you."

This is how I consoled myself, and put the abandonment behind me.

My relationship with Vlastos was a learning experience for me. I knew about the rejection of "others" all too well, but I had never experienced the rejection by someone I consider not "other," but a growing part of myself, a growing manifestation of my own heart. What I also learned was a new-found valuation of a university education. Now, life would be different. I began to yearn for more travels abroad, longer trips, more interesting and adventurous trips, far away from mediocrity and pedestrian associations.

I hate injections but that last one I had asked for. But from now on I would turn my backside to the needle with anticipation. I would only feel a slight sting now. Onward to Thessaloniki and Aristotle University.

The small old train chugged as it moved along the imperfectly linked sections of rails taking me to my new country, Thessaloniki, the bride of the Thermaic Gulf.

Chug, chug, the slow and antiquated train took hours and hours to get to the north of Greece; it stopped at every station and sometimes there seemed to be a mechanical breakdown and it stopped for hours. So we slept in the stinking compartment together with the chickens, the eggs, and the assorted foods most of the people carried with them. All manner of food and drink was allowed since the train offered nothing to eat or drink. We puffed on our cigarettes as if we were mimicking the old train itself; from afar I imagined us looking something like those films about East Africa where the trains are running in the middle of the plains amidst thousands of black and white people, immersed in a variety of colors, sounds, and smells, onlookers welcoming the long metallic leviathan at every station. Long endless conversations with fellow student immigrants and villagers along the route. Arriving never on time, always late.

Chugging, chugging, chugging, the train is running through the big valley of Thessaly, passing between the two giant mountain ranges of Olympus, the mountain of the Gods, and Kissavos, its modest companion, crossing over the big river of Pineios. This is how the immigrants feel when they travel by train to Germany, crossing the broad valleys that comprise the cores of so many European countries. Most of the immigrants pressed tight with their baggage in their small compartments, relegated to traveling by that super slow train which seemed at times as if it would never reach its destination.

Luckily it made it at the end...

Next to me, my mother was sitting, grumbling. That woman lacked patience. She loved traveling, but hated discomfort. I took after her, not in grumbling but in leaving, all the time leaving, departing with a suitcase in my hands. My life was well kept in a suitcase for the most fascinating journey, ever!

At last we arrived at the Thermaic Gulf and desperately put to the task of finding a house to reside — a roof beneath which my passions and florid aspirations could shelter. My life as a university student began in a tiny room which belonged to two crazy ladies, a woman and her single daughter. There was something peculiar about the room which did not appeal to me, but I readily overlooked it given the convenient location of the house directly next to the university.

My life as university student was directly corresponded to my experiences in Thessaloniki. My cohabitation with two lunatics soon became a torture, resulting in my being kicked out of their house. The stated reason was that I had peed on their mattress, rendering it moldy and putrid. They asked for compensation, but thanks to my mother and her genius friend I escaped from all that fuss, promising myself never to rent another room in that city. I had already been traumatized! Once was enough. I wanted to fly away, to escape. But how? I had succeeded in the exams of my first student's year and nothing but nothing tied me with that city anymore. I was planning to finish my studies via correspondence, being well equipped with brochures and notes from the lectures of our professors by two of my mates who had become my friends.

I felt like I wanted to escape from Thessaloniki. I was longing for something else. I felt like a bum, scruffy and duff, a fourth-rate species. I had always had that opinion about myself — kind of useless. I did not make any special effort to adjust myself to the status quo in Thessaloniki; on the contrary, I was expecting to be integrated by default — I cannot say by whom, to be recruited in a way. But this had not happened and I sort of kept my distance from everything that bothered. I abandoned my roots, altered my destination, and I was now riding my unbridled imagination to places that I could not reach in reality. I had been always yearning for something without knowing what exactly it was. I got anxious for unreasonable reasons and became stressed out about my expectations which I envisioned would stimulate and change my "ex parte."

SAINT GEORGIOS

My first something was the white bicycle and the rider, similar to Saint Georgios!

God bless that holy guy!

The dream of my adolescence became true. The one I had been chasing with my bicycle, the one I had in my colored dreams. The last dream was interrupted by my departure to America. Neither had I forgotten Georgis nor had he become an idea fixed or obsession. I was running after the experiences of my youth, and during reflective moments he materialized clearly in my dreams. Between us there has been that peculiar name of Vlastos who distracted me from Georgis, compelling me to keep him deeply into my heart for a while. He nested there, being transformed into a secret yearning, something like a private frustration, a half-finished story I never finished but which had to be brought to an end in the name of inner peace.

I had the feeling he did not make an effort to approach me. Along with his bicycle, he probably carried the same complexes similar to mine — complexes that were, at that time entirely consistent with his provincial way of thinking and behaving, rather conservative and restricted. On my part, there were some attempts to orchestrate an "accidental" meeting. Always according to the limits I set for myself lest he discovered my feelings and realized I was vigorously flirting with him. During that period in life such instances made me circumspect; in other words my thoughts and actions were constrained by my persisting valuation of the opinions of others in my life. Then...

"Let me talk, too. I think you talk too much...," Georgis said while recalling some memories:

"I met Zavolia riding her red bicycle up and down the whole village; the simple act of her doing so unsettled all the young boys as well as me. She must have been sixteen when I saw her for the first time passing by my father's butcher shop like a hurricane, carefree and easy-going, arrogant and distant, and perfectly oblivious of my standing at the door. She came from the capital city, Athens, 'a holiday maker' and those qualities belonged only to our long dreams. How could we dare, the young boys of a village, a provincial area with all its disadvantages to raise our eyes to such a lady? A stranger, like my mum used to say, as though she was coming from another planet: 'Don't you dare look at all those tourists, they come and go, don't let them hurt your feelings, and you never know what they are 'carrying' with them! I mean venereal diseases and all that stuff. Stay away, I'm warning you!'

"My mother was warning me, pointing her finger at me!

"I had a peculiar fear inside me which rendered me timid and was the source of continuous torment. The only thing I dared do — I, the poor guy — was to raise my bulging Negro eyes and look at her. There seemed little else I could do — increasingly immersed

in the puerile excitements of my adolescence, I was still recovering from the shame of having been kicked-to-the-curb by somebody else, I have heard!

"The thing I could do was to follow her everywhere on my bicycle and spy on her surreptitiously. Many times we 'accidentally' bumped into each other, exchanged a smile, and mutually blushed with lowered eyes. At those moments I wished that the earth would spontaneously split and instantly swallow me up whole. I was so dumb and shy.

"Time was passing. And like a cruel enemy it had been following us, became an obstacle in our way and we had been trying to fight it. For myself, I wished I had more guts to simply stop her in the middle of the road and tell her: 'I've seen you for some time from a distance, now I would like to get to know you better.'

"But the very thought of such spirit, seemed to set my innards ablaze and compelled me to shiver all over like those I had seen with Parkinson's disease.

"Then — for some unexplained reason — she vanished from the town. I was deranged by the sudden vacancy I had been thrust into — a vacancy I filled with spurned love and imagined jealousy. I tried to approach her brother. We were the same age and were both students, him at the Physics University in Athens and I at the Law University in Thessaloniki. We used to discuss student's problems, our lessons, and all the stuff young people talk about. But the principal reason I liked him was because he was her brother. I heard from him that Zavolia, my big love, was in the USA. A sense of suffocation fell over me upon hearing that she was gone, so far away, but I tried to be cool, not betraying my feelings to him.

"Blast, such a long distance, the other end of the world, another continent which swallowed most of the *kids all over the world. She would never come back. 'So, my story is over,' I thought.*

"My joy had instantly contorted itself into a knot that was seemingly trying choke me. The least I would do was maintain contact with her brother so as to be privy to the latest news concerning her. To those ends I promised myself to be more accessible and congenial in case we met again. But time had its own agenda and pace — one that was slow and glacial in its passing.

"A whole year passed away without seeing Zavolia, and then one brilliant day I heard from her brother that she had returned to Thessaloniki, that she had excelled in her exams in the Department of English Language and Literature. A blanketing comfort seemed to envelop me. At last, I would probably have a chance to see and talk with her again. Yet I had to do that before she went to Thessaloniki, because I was in the last year of my studies and I had to hurry back before I would lose her again.

"Good fortune smiled upon me one day I saw her at the beach in the company of a group of fellows, one of which was her brother. I seized the moment and went directly to her brother. Greeting everybody in the group, I was certain not to look directly at Zavolia. It was not long before they all took a dip in the sea, leaving her behind. Was it on purpose? I had to find out.

'Well, I heard from your brother that you passed the exams for the English Literature Department at the University of Thessaloniki. Congratulations! You know that I'm studying there at the Law Department.'

"I shared these facts as if she did not know anything about me.

'Exactly like that,' she said, rather indifferently.

"*I started shaking again, but I went on with renewed determination.*

'Whatever you need over there I can help you. I know that city so well. I've lived there almost five years now.'

'Do you still reside there?' She finally spoke the magic words.

'No, I gave the house back since I am on my diploma year and I have only to study and not to attend the lessons. I go up there only for the semester exams.'

'And where do you stay when you go there?' she asked again.

'At the hotel.'

'I see,' she replied.

"*Then one word followed the next, one phrase led to another, and it all concluded in me asking her out on a date.*

'What are you doing this afternoon?' I asked, just as her soaking brother emerged from the sea.

'The usual, nothing special,' she said.

'Would you like to go for a bicycle ride?'

'Why not, that's a good idea,' she said, with no apparent enthusiasm.

"*This is how I finally dated her. We took a long bicycle ride to another beautiful beach a little bit further from the village. Being somewhat the photographer, I brought my camera and took photos of her sitting on the rocks at sunset. When I asked to see her again the next day, she readily accepted. I had only touched her hand up to that point. I would have never dared to try something else, let's say a kiss...*"

"Can I go on now with the story?" Zavolia asked recalling some memories on her own:

"*Well, it was almost sunset when the next date started. Again on our bicycles, we had arranged to meet at Pefkakia, a picturesque beach lined with thousands of pine trees.*

"*He had brought his camera with him and he took so many photos of me. I thought I was a Hollywood star. Soon thereafter, in the dark of night, a soft light of a full moon that seemed to be lying on the tranquil sea illuminated our faces. It was a mythical night. We became moon-stricken. We had allowed so much time to pass without contact. This is how I thought then.*

'*Why didn't you speak to me all those years?*' *I asked him.*

'*I was dreading your rejection, your casual disregard,*' *he said sincerely.*

'*We let such a long time to pass by like that,*' *I said again.*

'*Now we've found it. Besides that you've been always well kept into my heart.*'

"*We started to date on a regular basis. Another relationship that was completely different from the previous one. My big first love. Georgis was an exceptional young man. Very special, very good looking with a fantastic body and an innocent and sensitive heart. While I was in Athens he wrote me letters that were precious pieces of literature to me from a man who seemed born to be a writer. I wonder now whether he still writes. He was well read, thousands of books on all topics, well informed about politics and social life, about literature and poetry. He seemed to know something about everything and his opinion counted to me. He opened another door in life for me and he graciously escorted me through it, deep into the world of books that I adored. Absorbed, we were, into literature, poetry, short stories, politics, social research. There was so much inside of me that had been looking to be lifted to the surface by a welcoming hand to be. Although shy and timid, he was both a very good speaker and listener. He even seem to hear your private feelings, the words you were ready to speak but didn't, your wishes, your desires. Tender and sensitive he was, a man who seemed to admire me the way I was. He took great pride in my being alongside him, as if I were an idol next to the ugliness he saw himself to be!*

"Even our psychological complexes seemed to intertwine. A perfect mixture!

"The cod liver oil that my mother used to give me to fortify my constitution was suddenly rendered pointless in light of Georgis. He was all the tonic that I needed, having become the best therapeutic injection of self-confidence and esteem ever...!

"We met in the nice cozy apartment that Georgis' family had in downtown Athens. We would go to the movies, to the theatre, to the pubs and cafeterias, we made long walks in the Plaka and under the Acropolis, we sat on the benches, we visited exhibitions, we went to pub-restaurants, those fantastic places with Greek artistic music where a new style of music was slowly rising up onto the Greek stage — music where poetry was turned into songs. Music that seemed to inspire, police round-ups after midnight due to the revolutionary lyrics that were not complimentary of the Papadopoulos Junta.

'Lydra' was one of them. When the police came inside they stopped the whole performance, they arrested people, they kicked them out with the clubs. I was so scared, although it had never happened during our visit there, but we had heard all about it. Of course, after a while they reopened Lydra and once

again they started singing. Georgis told me not to be afraid given my inability to run, for if the police returned for another round of violence he could take me into his arms or upon his shoulders and we would escape. His words made me so happy. On the one hand I was scared like hell because I could not endure a beating, and on the other hand I was so happy imagining me escaping from the police in the arms of Georgis. Very romantic!

"*And never forget those fantastic trips to Thessaloniki, Georgis!*

"*Do you remember? Never together. Being well off, you went by plane. Me — by train, being poor and subject to plane sickness! You were waiting for me at the train station. We met there. I slept at my friend's house and you went to your hotel, and we met in hidden corners and obscure alleys since we wanted to keep our relationship secret from our parents. My mother, the smart fox, had been very suspicious of my movements of late, having noticed the distinct changes in my demeanor. Her suspicions were confirmed when some of the village gossip-mongers conveyed to her what they had seen of our clandestine meetings.*

"*Since she had set herself the task to follow me around like a detective, dropping on my phone calls, at times speaking to Georgis harshly. Such a pity that at the time mobile phones had not yet been invented. Every time I was dressed nicely for the purpose of going out with my friends — my alibi — she started shouting hysterically and gesticulating like a lunatic!*

"*It had taken me such a longtime to find such a good injection of sorts for my health, and now she was corrupting its effects were her madness.*

"She was not fond of 'cheer-up' injections at all, that lady!

"I can imagine a film shot with my mother as the featured star; it revolved around her incessant snooping, pursuit of Georgis and I in taxis, at times with her hair in shiny rollers like a rocket. It would have been such a funny film!

"When I finally reached your place I told you my story, prompting us to burst into tearful laughter upon recounting my mother's deeds. Our best, our happiest!

"But it did scare you. I noticed this fear and your desire to be free from the entanglements of family drama. You were right!

"One night when I returned home, the same imaginary film was being screened, her grumbling and provocative quips were met by my calm demeanor as I promptly passed by on the way to bed. Bidding her 'good night,' I closed the door on her acrimonious glare.

"Years later, when you and I met again, we recalled those moments and we laughed again... Just as we once had."

A great station on the path of my life was Georgis. An important reprieve, an opportunity to recharge my batteries before sallying forth!

Georgis the first, Andre who came in my forties. Both of them stimulated my life, beyond my expectations and limits. I do not think that I will find such points of significance in my life again. Most stations on the trajectory of my life have long been vulgarized by the sterility of modernity, none of them retains any semblance of the local and traditional aesthetics of days past. "Modernity" is increasingly synonymous with the intensely unbearable.

Metal drowns me and glass makes me cold!

The rest of the story, like most love stories and affairs, is not uncommon. We had been dating for about two years. Then, after he was awarded his diploma, he had to serve in the army. He went to Crete where he sent me intensely literate love letters. An important relationship...but without a future! Somewhere in the middle of the course of our affections we took different paths. We were so young, lost in searching the meaning of life, following our visions. We had set our goals and yearned to conquer.

> *Before my eyes you've been light,*
> *Before love you've been love,*
> *And when the first kiss overwhelmed you,*
> *A woman.*

These were the last words in one of Georgis' letters just prior to our separation. Using the great verses of Odysseas Elytis, our Nobel Prize poet, he had expressed his feelings. Through poetry, he let a part of his soul emerge. That was a charm that seemed particularly native to our private rapport. We had been searching our inner selves through art and we experienced art in our daily life.

EFFECTIVE INJECTIONS

The next "something" went by the name of *Encyclopedia Giovanis*.

My first cousin, Christos, who had loose nerves like mine, was a genius, inventive and hardworking guy, creative with dreams and ambitions. He had scarcely managed to graduate from public school with the worst grades when he undertook the representation of *Encyclopedia Giovanis*, newly released to the Greek market. In content it was the worst quality but it was supposed to be sold by any means. He established his own office downtown and was seeking salesmen. He trained them for a while before releasing them to generate sales; He had sent them into the wolf's lair or into deep dark water where they would have to swim to seek their personal fortune without a life preserver.

"Eh, what do you think, you smart angel," he told me one day.

"Do you want to make some money?"

Christos and I had grown up together. He was two years younger than me but he nevertheless was a man of miracles. Very capable and a sharp brain like a knife! There was a special relationship developing between us; we secretly admired and appreciated each other. We talked directly, free of insinuation.

It was during my student years in Thessaloniki with the lunatic ladies where I was trying to escape from. That solution came from heaven. That's why I dared to try it in that selling field as well.

"I'll come. Where am I going to work?" I asked him.

"Everywhere! Around Greece! Money and experiences along with tales," he said while winking roguishly.

We had spent most of our adolescence in the village of Georgis where our holiday houses were next to each other. Together we had built our respective sets of summer companions where we collectively celebrated our teen-age dreams. Together we had experienced our first ventures into romantic love, our first searching for recognition, our first parties at the beach, impassioned hearts, and our first experimentation in the joys of drinking to excess.

One of those summer nights in that holiday resort we were coming back home from a wonderful party drinking ouzo. We had to walk a distance of about a kilometer to our house. Every night we went out, once to eat souvlaki, then to drink coffee, then for ouzo and wine, then to dance at the local clubs, flirting all the while, and having the first experience of our platonic loves.

We were a combination of locals and holiday-makers of about the same age who were having a great time during summer. In the morning we went swimming till noon, sometimes until the afternoon, and at night we raided the various local clubs and bars. In other words, we were enjoying our life!

One of my weaknesses was the simple act of walking, which tired me more rapidly than the others. It compelled me to frequently stop to gather myself.

"Come, climb up on my shoulders," Christos said, bending down so that I could climb up. He held my hands so I wouldn't fall as I sat upon his shoulders.

"Don't worry," I told him. "I'll hold your head or I can lean on your head."

"Watch out and don't pull my hair," he warned me.

We were all so drunk that night, a state of intoxication adrenalized by constant laughter that allowed us to experience our youth without inhibitions. While walking, he was making great zigzags, staggering and laughing without any reason at all, like a lunatic. I, sitting on the mast of his boat, was reacting the same way, laughing with tears of joy. Suddenly, I felt an urgent need to go to the toilet.

"Christos, can you walk faster?" I asked him as sweetly as I could, knowing how unpredictable his reactions were.

"Donkeys cannot run with such a heavy load," he said to me as he started braying and bucking like a donkey.

"Hee aww, hee haww, hee hawwwwwww," he blurted out while breathing heavily.

Holding onto his head to hang on, I was about to fall off when by accident I pulled his hair.

"Ah, ah, ah, why are you pulling my hair, you witch, you are going to uproot it. Hey, what are you doing? Are you crazy? Can't you pull something else instead of my hair?"

He started laughing again.

My necessity to go to the toilet became stronger.

"Christos, you know something, I have to pee right now. Can't you hurry up a little bit?"

I had hardly spoken the words when I found myself on the ground. He had pushed my legs away and he let me fall without warning and without thinking of the consequences of my falling.

"Plaf!"

My body made a terrible thud. I thought I had broken something. But thank God I got up and everything was all right. Unfortunately the same could not be said about my pants which were already wet. I had peed unwillingly my pants.

My paranoid and attractive cousin, Christos!

So I trusted my cousin absolutely. I soon started working somewhere on the outskirts of Thessaloniki, northern Greece. It was by then when we went to Thrace. To tell you the truth, I felt a bit embarrassed in the beginning. A saleswoman with special needs, a handicapped saleswoman. Such a peculiar sight to see! My new role in the theatre of the paranoids, a wandering circus troupe of the absurd.

I undertook the responsibility of a group. He spoke and I obeyed. So I became a group manager, which meant I was in charge of a group of five people that included myself. I had recently got my driving license for a car that had been specifically converted for handicapped people. Automatic cars by that time were not imported in Greece.

That was the gift of my father who was pensioned and had received his compensation as a result of working so many years. The car was a Renault Dacia which he had desperately tried to learn to drive without success. So he gave it to me. At that time my brother was serving in the army and could not object to such a gift being given to me. I "loaded" my company of salesmen in that car and off we went to earn our fortune selling second-hand goods in Thrace, and ultimately to extend to all the villages and small towns of Greece. An encyclopedia in twelve volumes. Although it had to be sold, I had no idea how.

This is what my cousin ordered us to do.

A broad and undisciplined mind was he!

I and my team of salesmen started looking for our treasure as soon as we landed on the "Treasure Island" called Volos, somewhere in the north.

We visited peoples' houses in the early afternoon since we cared that their children should be at home. We spent hours and hours in making our sales pitch using every marketing trick that we knew.

The marketing seminars we attended at my cousin's office were of little value upon facing reality inside the houses of clients, talking to the people and trying to persuade them to buy. I was learning very fast. In the beginning I was shy, then I gradually became so persistent and persuasive that I couldn't believe my progress. Ultimately I would not leave the house unless I had sold the encyclopedia. We all learned fast and after a while we became top salesmen. We were born salesmen as we figured out later on.

What we had earned during daylight, we spent it at twilight.

We had visited all the small tsipouro and ouzo places, sampling hundreds of dishes, each with a distinctive flavor.

Experiencing my first successes in sales compelled me to grow up at a dangerous pace. My capacity to sell always seemed to exceed my expectations. It was a hidden talent I had never realized. I was tremendously good! This is what a father told me once while I was making a sale in his house: "You are tremendously good, you've already exhausted us all here. If I could, I would have bought two encyclopedias because of your grace. You are something, you lady. Well done!"

Now I was soaring in the air. Nobody and nothing could have brought me down! Spectacular flying tricks I was doing in the air with my super Fandom airplane. When I knocked on the customers' door, they half opened it and then I put my foot in the gap to keep it open. Normally I used my weak leg; once an angry guy almost smashed it trying to close the door.

Such behaviors I dared to repeat, again and again. I did not care at all. I wanted only to get inside the house, begin my pitch, and make the sale. Only sell. That was the target! I put on my best smile, put honey in my mouth, and as soon as I had penetrated their private kingdom, the castles were attacked and after an hour or three the people surrendered to my wit. What was, at first, hesitation to interact with me and my team soon turned into a happy family gathering, and often an invitation to dinner. We were friendly and flattering. After the great victory, I proceeded to limp towards the battlements of the next castle.

After a while I was practically the best salesman of our group.

After a month I had sold many encyclopedias. My growing fame was increasingly the subject of gossip. I became a first class saleswoman. Incredible but real, this whole period of success would soon fade from my consciousness as my life continued on to other things. I never returned to my studies in Thessaloniki. I had sworn an oath! That was the end of my life as a student. I had already entered another world — the world of the working class. Mostly, I enjoyed it, earning good money, which of course was immediately spent on the dalliances of a single night. But most notably was the effect on my psyche, for my confidence rose tremendously and that soaring sense of self pushed me away from my "problem." Something strong was happening inside me, a transformation that was palpably evident in my demeanor, but a transformation with an end point that was still obscure to me. It would take the ripening of time to show me the path!

The next restorative, and effective injection into my life was the male sex. Arsenic poisoning it is called in the Greek language, however the profile of masculinity in my life was not poisonous at all, on the contrary it was refreshing and regenerating; whether that man was young, middle aged, older, illiterate, literate, boring or interesting, attractive or flat, privileged and talented, or the contrary was irrelevant. There were more males in our sales team than females, that's why the practice of salesmanship became easier for me. The masculine gender often represented a stinging and hurtful injection at times, but it overwhelmingly did me good. Sometimes, the fluid of the injection was not well dissolved, having congealed into an embolus that would hurt. It compelled me to apply wet and warm compresses so that the embolus would dissipate faster. Another struggle taking place! Another battle — that of coexistence with the male sex. It was a mandatory treatment in order to reach the desired cure!

A whole life full of injections on my buttocks because of my physical rehabilitation! When I was hearing the door bell ringing I tried to hide in order to avoid the injection. Then I started crying. I took my revenge by passing on the same injections onto my poor doll, to my pillow, even to my younger cousins. Now the new "male injections" were about my psychological well-being. I was yearning for the latest brand! Although they hurt sometimes, they were absolutely effective. I found out as time passed I was increasingly recovering quicker and quicker, something was going on inside me, for my own good. I stopped fighting with my "whys" and started chasing only my "wishes."

The ingredients of those injections were very simple. One warm smile, a quick glare, a smart compliment, a joke, a touch, a kiss, an unexpected feeling and a nice word of solace. I started liking my incredible me, the way it was, the way it looked, with all my defects and defaults. I felt something fascinating happening inside me. I felt my aura circulating in people's blood, flying up in the air. I started fancying my own body, at last. I looked myself in the mirror without shame, and I liked me. I embraced me, I patted me, I felt at last proud of myself because I found Me being beautiful. I felt beautiful. Almost loving me the way I was!

Let's take a selfie then!

The injections were miraculous. An energetic field, the whole me attracting and charming people without great effort. I was getting well without special remedies. The miracle I was expecting was taking place. I went to bed without asking "why?" I woke up without question marks. I was singing, warbling, and trilling like a happy bird flying away from its cage. My wings were now growing fast and more spectacularly every day and I dared to explore the art of flying ever higher and further afield.

Second station, Macedonia, to be followed by other cities or small towns; Grevena, Kozani, Siatista, Florina, Chalkidiki, Veria, Giannitsa, Serres, Drama and, at the end, Thrace, Ferres, Alexandroupolis, Didymoteicho, Kastanies, Soufli where we left an encyclopedic trail of success. Every town, every village, every big city was a station for resting, the endeavors to a new existence.

Just because we were next to the north borders of the country there were many military camps with a lot of soldiers serving their duty.

We met them frequently at the small tavernas where we had dinner at the end of the day. They were listening to sad songs while dancing passionately under the frustrating melodies, recruited to the altar of their country who washed them and drained them like swollen corpses there next to the Turkish villages far away from their homes and habits, right on the borderline of the horizons where Greece ended and Turkey and Bulgaria began; at the borders to guard the Greek territory who turned them from the one night to the other into men.

> *Come and join us soldier,*
> *Sit down and have a drink with us,*
> *Forget about barracks and guard duty,*
> *And drink from dry wine of our heart…*

The song was playing on the juke-box.

Intermingling ourselves with them, we became one body and one soul. We shared our sorrow and bitterness, our homesickness, we felt conscripts in the army of our own country, taking part in their desperate dancing with a small wine glass in our hands. The least we could do was to watch the frenetic explosion of their instincts from a distance, the last attempt of their suffering bodies to overcome the difficulties and the heavy burdens of their obligatory service.

In the morning, they were once again in camp, ready and clean, with stiff posture ready for inspection without any traces of the cathartic labors of the previous day. On duty, on the arms, sleepless guards of the Greek borders.

The border of Greece and Turkey at this point was the broad river Evros.

Majestic and superb! Its nobility in its look! I sat by its banks and as I was watching it, I boasted about its appearance. I looked to the other side to find a sign that differentiated the two races of people that it separated. Nature gave no indication of any such division. Everything was the same. Only the ungainly flying of the stork disturbed the tranquil water. The magnificent and monstrous river, another sleepless sentry of our country's perimeter, an untamed wild animal when it swelled and poured over its banks to simultaneously vanquish animals and the agricultural labors of months in a singular night, making no distinction between native and foreigner, or friend and enemy.

Thrace, the praised and the pained one, the Cinderella province, the mother who sustained everybody, who embraced all the miseries and sorrows of the refugees, living always under threat of incursion. Over the centuries Thracians have remained innocent and untouchable, resistant to the fortunes that befell the remainder of our race; steeped in their traditions which have long conveyed elements of the bitterness and sorrow attending their isolation from the Hellenic core. Their traditional fiestas and dances did not extol joy and happiness but rather a quiet acrimony and acquiescence to the status quo that gave no hint of impending change, revolution, or rebirth for esteem and import that had long evaporated into history. The noble aristocrats of the borderlands, the bold merchants, the proud and lofty Pashas.

Didymoteicho... Didymoteicho Blues... The twin towers of Kale, where I had walked through stone by stone, touching them with my palms. I peered over the hills and disappeared into the great valleys between them. I walked through the narrow picturesque streets of the town with the prominent Turkish architectural flavors of the ethnic quarters. The house of the nobles with the front and back yards, like the basements full of goods, were seemingly untouched by time. Even the houses of the poor boasted an austere nobility linked to their poverty. All of them neat and comfortable, tidy and clean, seemingly expecting the unexpected visitor any time, any minute. Friendly and hospitable, disinterested and pure, innocent and purified by the mud their adored and beloved river Evros debagged their life and their grave too.

On the one side there stood and ran that grandiose and magnificent river Evros with its brackish water offsetting the saltwater of the Thracian Sea which cut into the heart of the big river in frustration. Alexandroupolis, on the one side, the metropolis of Thrace lying next to the mouth of the giant river and on the other side across the borders the remote and grandiose Andrianoupolis. Once upon a time it was Greek...

The houses of Thrace we visited to sell our products were so warm and hospitable that we felt so much at home that we often refused to leave. The lords of those houses offered us the best they had in their cupboards as well as lagers in abundance. Home-made wine, tsipouro and snaps, sweets with the aroma of cinnamon and vanilla, delicious cooked food with a fine flavor. We were enjoying their hearty hospitality, seated on the couches among the big embroidered and comfortable pillows. They treated us like friends with love and not as the strangers, the salesmen, who intruded upon their privacy in order to sell products. Sugared almonds, very fine tastes, fine flavors, fine aroma, fine communication, strong feelings in a small town of northern Greece forgotten by the rest of the world, isolated, remote and removed from the history and wiped off the map; yet a noble world of colors, sounds, images, paintings, pure nature which retained its own history and tradition against any hostile or peaceful invasion.

Horestias, Soufli, the last station, Kastanies, next to the steaming breath of the Bulgarian border guards. We perused their silk and web garments, their fine embroideries and the handcraft artistic creations of the women of north Thrace. We walked again along the cobbled stone narrow streets and pavements, we listened to their distinctive melodies.

When the time came for our visit to end, the prospect of leaving that charming town brought us to tears. The personal bonds we had forged, however brief they may have lasted, had become strong and intense. We had become a part of their town, a part of their society notwithstanding the fact that we went there to sell and cheat them, to sell questionable knowledge and problematic chronicles of 'history' to the unaware. Even, inadequate!

We, the small bandits...

They, the great nobles...

They felt they had to buy the encyclopedia. It was like an inner impulse to be grateful to somebody. To seal up our newly born friendship! This is how they felt. Amazing! I think the word "filotimo," which means "honor my friend," portrays a mixed feeling of dignity and pride. That exists only in the Greek vocabulary. There does not seem to be a corresponding word in the best dictionaries of the more prominent languages of the world.

In Thrace we had sold so many encyclopedias not because the region was wealthy but rather because they liked us so much. We were the best of the best, with good manners, humor, skill, and the most important of all, we were capable of communicating with all kinds of people.

We stayed there about three months. The market there was an endless source of energy, an energetic field boiling but not exploding. It contained the wealth of the whole world.

Three years I spent selling books throughout Greece. I wandered throughout the entire country, everywhere, nothing was left behind, and nothing was forgotten. This is how I got to know my own country, through its simple and pure people, where tradition and history co-existed, retaining a perfect relationship with each other, and where different races had found the right pace of life to move in unison. The winning lotto ticket of my life up to that point, the best public school I ever experienced. Three amazing and fantastic years of my life were dedicated to this form of my self-development.

The golden age!

In the beginning when I had started my work in sales, I was only a small fish opening and closing its mouth continuously swimming into that narrow bowl with water where small fishes are kept as pets in the house.

Soul of a fish in a lion's body! Later on would be transformed into a royal lion, with blond mane and a huge mouth with sharp teeth, a real beast of prey, which mangled all obstacles in its path.

No hesitation, no mercy, only daring, walking ahead to regain lost time. There we were, the group manager and the salesmen. We had very capable and skillful salesmen who were versatile, four to five sales per day. Adventurers and fortune-seekers; gold-diggers with the spirit of Marco Polo. We lived for today. The word "tomorrow" did not exist in our vocabulary. We all became friends and learned to share common feelings and experiences. We entertained ourselves at night at the best taverns and fiestas of the area, eating, drinking, singing and dancing, but mostly traveling into our lonely souls as well as into other new places to purchase our goods. Each of us a unique story!

Seekers of money and new countries, seemingly aristocratic and noble in the dignity of our commercial mission.

We had been moving back and forth of the regional landscape of southeastern Europe, slowly drawn back to our roots, to our own soils. We could smell the distinctive aroma of our own lands. We had placed our life onto a casual and temporary basis, and we allowed chance to chart our path. Acrobats and jugglers, arrivistes and climbers.

**

Giovanis' Circus
Spectacular and grandiose
Come and see us all

"Come in, come in, people, the headless body, the acrobat, the juggler, rich scenery, a variety of roundabouts, our clown, the iron chains are for free, the fatal jumping only two cents or two eggs instead, a majestic performance for young and old..."

**

Our wandering well-equipped circus, a great spectacle for young and old. We erected our sets, donned our costumes and stepped out onto the stage. We laughed and cried along with the audience and harmonized with their various moods. We got into their skin and burrowed beneath their souls. At the end of the performance we put the scenery down again, we took off our costumes and receded once again into our personal anonymity. No more acrobatics in empty dreams, no more gambling, heads or tails, our life...? We might perform some somersaults only to warm up ourselves till the next performance. At day's end we lowered our head down onto the cold linen of a provincial hotel bed awaiting the next daylight that clings to the eternal insecurity of life.

I was deeply sank into the strange and unknown, the new world you want to conquer and explore and learn something about it. We had been walking on the pavement of life, being conscious to avoid the deep ditches. We never walked on big roads and avenues. We were afraid of them. This was a rite of passage of sorts, necessary to advance to the next stage of life that we had thought we had always been destined for.

Most of our salesmen were university students like me who had been searching and testing themselves, others without either education or future plans. However they tended to be the first class salesmen because they deposited their souls in the name of the present and profit. They were most daring and effective, of course. Those were the flyers, the pilots, the visionaries. Uncompromised and rebellious always gone…

We were a traveling "Tower of Babel." Each one of us spoke a different language. However the common language united us and we got along very well together, an Esperado, a hope, leading us to our common dreams and goals. Hard working and profitable. For three whole years I had been having those amazing injections till my poor buttocks became so swollen, all without a doctor's prescription. For three years I had earned for me, I've yearned for me, I've tried hard to fix me and restore me, to improve me, to integrate me into the society of the "capable."

I was so fed up, so sick and tired of that pattern. My academic credentials that I had long neglected during this impromptu sortie into commercialized self-development was calling me back. How? I seemingly now was residing on another planet there was no way back. Working and fighting for my own existence along with the God of romantic Love with its magic wings flying and tempting. A re-orientation to my real goals had moved front and center. Another hard effort was at hand..!

THE CUFF

Even though the doctors in America had declared, "no more injections, no more medication, no more iron braces," I ignored their advice and I went on not only with the injections but I started taking iron supplements so at to increase my physical fortitude!

Science was progressing and I was looking for more improved and advanced injections, like a piece of modern technology I sought out better upgrades to advance my abilities beyond the limitations of ordinary humanity.

I was seemingly on the verge of a complete personal reparation, restoration, rehabilitation, all without needing anymore the Rehab Center I'd graduated from. That nightmare!

Yes, I had been an institutional inmate — but that was long ago. This time I was going to establish my own institution for the physical and mental rehabilitation of young people. A sanity-and-body-curing center with a cosmopolitan flair. Again in the provinces, far away from big cities! Athens, my birthplace — where I took my first steps and matured — is kicking me out to smaller or foreign locales, to either illuminate them or set them on fire...!?

Finally I got my degree from the Aristotle University of Thessaloniki. It had taken me longer than projected due to a phlegmatic and narrow-minded British professor who taught poetry. Like so many of his discipline, he sought to uproot the poetry from the hearts of his students. After the tenth semester I succeeded in his course and I finally graduated! But I graduated with somewhat of a broken heart since I had had been having an affair for the final two years with Tassos, sharing his family house along with his widowed mother. Tassos was our new very capable and intelligent group manager, a gallant and arrogant guy from the Pontos region. My suspicious past defined my new position in our small community. While I persisted on, I was in fact gone already, flying to the south, I wanted to change my life, the sooner the better.

Farewell to arms, the primitive ones, now I needed weapons of the latest and newest technology for my survival under new terms and conditions, nuclear, atomic and damned devastating. There was no other way.

Complete transformation.

I abandoned the poor countries of the North and all my good friends and colleagues, that amazing and adventurous traveling troupe of salesmen, I said goodbye to my last love, cried over the ashes of that relationship, and I headed for the South. A new country for me, though familiar... We had been crying all together over our last "goodbye," afterwards we made no effort to preserve our fellowship since most of us were emotionally gone, already traveling and growing away from our common dreams and goals. Life was calling us ahead, for new surprising super-flights.

It was I who departed first longing to set foot on native soil.

A happy family reunion after a long time! Triumph, pride and emotion because of my university degree. My dear father was crying and he wished me good luck. He was the one who had noticed the transformation in me and was so happy.

"I am so proud of you. Now, I am not scared of death since I saw the light coming out of you. You seem like a fireball, happy. I apologize I've underestimated you. You are a very strong person my dear daughter and I admire you for that. Now, I know that you don't need me anymore."

"I need your love and support to go on. I've learned so much from you. You pushed me ahead and I am grateful to you. You did not try to hide my handicap in a fake marriage but you showed me another way of self-respect and esteem, the only way to emancipation and independence. You showed me how to love myself and make the best out of it. Thanks, daddy!"

I put tenderly my arms around him and pinned my kiss on his right cheek.

I stayed there still for a while, breathing the smell of his skin, his manly after-shave cologne with lemon, tears forming in my eyes. I was not alone after all...

After the first hugs and kisses, and the new impressions, my sweet mother started grumbling once again. My brother was there too, having finished serving in the Greek army, he was preparing to get married. I loved my family but returning to them brought with it a feeling of imprisonment of sorts. I immediately felt the need to escape again, scrambling frantically in any direction, like a lunatic, seeking my salvation. Another getaway was boiling in my blood.

I found a part-time teaching job in a private school for foreign languages. It was spring. A friend of mine was teaching there and she was going to give birth to her child. I accepted the position with mixed feelings, happiness and fear. I had never worked before with children and teenagers. I knew nothing about their sensibilities. I was carrying the traumatic experiences of my past which caused me to hesitate somewhat to exposing myself to the discomforting critiques children and teenagers often indulged in.

But I overcame it and I endured my baptism into the world of teaching.

Such a fantastic experience! Teenagers; easy going and full of energy.

I felt the same way, too. There was an immediate mutuality between us, creative and enjoyable at the same time. The first lessons were lots of fun. Then the owner of the school proposed to continue my employment for the following school year. I delayed responding to this request, but I did not immediately refuse. My utmost wish was to work at the 'public' schools rather than a private one. To work in the public schools one had to prepare a paper as part of the application process and remain on the waiting list for about three or four years. However, the wishes of mere people are not always heard by Gods...

The first big slap, smack, rejection and disaster! My first attempt to work in a public school was disastrous. I had to pass through the Health Committee of our Health and Social Security Ministry. There I realized again that I was handicapped, crippled, invalid, disabled; all those fantastic adjectives to distinguish me from the anonymous masses. I had actually forgotten that I was readily seen in terms of one of these adjectives as I stood in front of the five members of the Idiots Committee. They decided my fate with one thought and one voice: I was an inappropriate teacher for a public school. And not only that. They also concluded that I represented a risk and danger for public health and the viability of the social security system. The public declaration and decision by all voting members of the Idiot Doctors Committee was that I was incapable, invalid, and handicapped.

"According to Law bla, bla, bla, where it was stated, instead of throwing you down the Keadas cliff and also having to pay for the bus ticket to Sparta, we set you free so you can do it yourself in case you feel like it, since you are also so useless, wrong and unsuitable for the education of the public!!!"

A sad episode which made me very furious and bitter, but I overcame it since I had already escaped from my invalid body. I had entered a new healthy body.

However by the moment I passed through the door of that terrible and ugly room of the Health Ministry department I had the first big shock of my life and I felt the earth slipping under my feet, me ready to collapse. My blood was so panicked and wanted to escape out of my veins running fast till the edges of my fingers and toes. To abandon me without mercy.

"Why did you study?" one of the idiot doctors asked me.

"Pardon, sir?" I asked as though I had not heard very well.

"I said, why did you study?"

"Should I have sought your permission before I went to study at the university?"

"Of course, be well informed and know your rights since there was not a chance even in the million to get a post in the public school. We work according to the letter of the law. What do you think?"

"I think you don't think well. Something is wrong with all of you here."

"Maybe you are not well. And that is, of course, apparent to the eye. Normally kids make fun when they see something strange and weird, something odd."

"I beg your pardon, sir? Did you call me strange and weird, odd you mean?"

I started boiling with anger and emotion.

"Generally speaking, the kids are merciless. That's why the government laid down such laws to protect you from being ridiculed and humiliated in public."

"Right now I am humiliated by you, the State's representatives! That's enough! Why should I be ridiculed in public school? What do you mean, sir? I assure you I am very well respected by my students."

Another doctor on the committee spoke up.

"Well, to tell you the truth I wouldn't have any objection to you teaching privately — even with my own kids, although you are handicapped. There would be no problem. It's different though in the public school. Working with the masses is another thing, you see. We wish to protect our civilians. That's the reason we make laws."

"Have you undergone a lobotomy or something before being assigned to the Public Health Insurance System, sir?" I asked him.

I was shocked and mostly influenced by Ken Kesey's book "One Flew Over the Cuckoo's Nest." According to the author there were inhuman surgeries performed on people's living organs, normally the brain in the expectation of transforming the patient into a normal and obedient citizen. These surgeries were performed on dissidents and drop-outs who were deemed in need of being tamed in order to conform to authority.

I knew I was talking nonsense to the committee but I was so overwhelmed by this terrible encounter. It wasn't myself but somebody else who was crying and shouting and swearing at them in that terrible and miserable room. It was so unfair.

The committee foreman spoke forthrightly.

"I think you are out of your mind! You talk nonsense. We are trying to save you from public humiliation and you repay our concern by shouting at us?"

"You know who you are? Doctors selected from the garbage of the Greek public health system. You must be ashamed of yourselves the way you treat me. Shame on you. You consider yourselves scientists!? But what can we expect from such a country with a military government? Leadership? This government is manipulating us. And you are its servants. Shame on you."

I spat again on the floor scornfully instead of spitting right there in their ugly and evil faces. I felt desperate and hurt.

"Kick her out, the rude communist. Instead of paying more attention to her terrible situation, her handicap, she is trying to give us lessons about our way of thinking and acting. Kick her out! Kick her out before we call the police to arrest her!"

They were shouting and nodding at me. They had become furious and aggressive, and wanted to shoot me right there in the middle of that terrible room because I was claiming equal rights as a normal citizen. The worst form of racism in my life. Till then, by my own people. I had an idea about racism in America but I had no idea it applied for people with disabilities too. A fascistic practice, the subject of much Nazi propaganda.

I might have been kicked out violently because when I recovered from the great shock I was in front of the elevator and somebody was opening the door for me and was pushing me inside.

Inside the lift I collapsed. I almost fainted, but not quite.

"Damn it, am I so different from other people? Is that why they treat me like I'm so dangerous? Why have I forgotten all about it?"

I was blaming myself.

"You dummy, you had thousands of injections, that's why you've deleted that from your memory... Yet the problem still exists. Do you hear that?"

Selfie was answering me.

"Well, I thought that the injections were curing me. Not just repressing the distasteful."

"Nothing is ever completely healed. Besides that, the healing process is slow and it takes a long time. And you know what? There is always something left at the end, a defect, a default, a blemish you have to carry on your shoulders, forever. Bear that in mind!"

Selfie was opposing me.

I was so strict and severe with my image. I did not like Selfie at all!

I blamed it for my condition.

Whether blemish or defect, default or handicap, I had already been flying far away, from all those imbecile servants of our famous public system. I wiped off my tears and I became active again. I turned me "on" and I experienced myself in another career, one that was ostensibly far from public education. I started looking in the newspaper about a job as a teacher. I was looking for something else. I did not even want to work for that small private school in Athens that I had worked for previously. I wanted to get away from Athens again. Escape from my destiny. Whether the classified ads was the right way to get a job, I did not know. Upon applying, I simply said nothing about my handicap. That was kept as a surprise. If they liked me they would have liked me the way I was, otherwise they would reject me.

Finally, I found a teaching job to work away from the big city, Athens, albeit the very humble wage. The job was not at all profitable but I wanted it like hell if just to, once again, "escape."

I was sent to Orchomenos, a town near Delphi and the beautiful mountain of Parnassos. Aside from the mountain and one of the richest valleys in the area, the small town was flat, wet and ugly. As farmers are apt to do, local society entirely revolved around the practice of agriculture. There I found out that the whole business with the ads was about a fake company with bandits and cheaters working only to make money out of the parents. A teacher, in that case it was me, would be sent to an obscure locale to secure a building and furnishings. Both pupils and parents would also be compelled to pay in advance for the courses and by the time everything was settled that band of bandits disappeared.

But, they were good for me, since I took advantage of my good chances and prospects and I got into work like a maniac to establish my being and a good name over there. In the beginning, I went to work for two months in the summer time since the courses were intensive, in July and August but I finally stayed there for seven years!

A whole life seeming very adventurous in the beginning but becoming very interesting and prosperous after some time!

I worked there those two months in the midst of a terrible heat and humidity. I was so beloved and accepted by the pupils and the local society that I founded my own private school after the first year, which became the most famous institute for foreign languages, English in the beginning, and later on, French. "The grand school," as they called it.

That school was the greatest school of my life. There I learned everything about my teaching job, since I was learning through working and attending seminars and courses that were directly applicable to the practice of my job. Every weekend I went to Athens to find out more about my work, the books, the ways of teaching and the practical problems of running your own business. I was learning faster than the kids because I liked the job and I wanted to expand my knowledge and experiences, as well as continuously increase the body of students that were being served.

Besides my professional life, my personal life was much improved.

Now I was a business woman with a lot of activities, well respected and appreciated by the local society and beyond. My reputation was growing throughout the region. My students passed their exams and received their diplomas by the means of my own small school. They continued their studies in Athens or abroad. My development in the professional field was ascending, spectacular and profitable. At last I felt like a normal person being integrated into the world of the "healthy ones"!

* *

Issue 5. Periodical informative magazine for the citizens

In our next issue coming to the public next week, we are informed that Zavolia was finally cured. According to scientific data and detailed medical examinations, we are informed that she was completely cured, having been well-attended-to in the famous Rehabilitation Centre of Nowhere. She is coming back to her new house, in Maroussi, a bit further on from her family house, to live alone. A cozy and comfortable apartment she has rented on the fourth floor of a newly built construction and in the most beautiful suburb of Athens. She wants to stay alone, far away from all those peculiar and strange people, shepherds, cowboys, farmers and butchers, animals and crops, and she wants to start a new life in the public school, as a civil servant. She is public, which means metaphorically, cheap and stale. Everything belonging to the public is something rough, contemporary, cut-rate, poorly constructed, rudely treated, a public road full of ditches, a public building comprised of police-style interrogation rooms. She is not seeking for publicity, having been publicly rejected, publicly exhibited, a public place herself, and a public toilet, which means stinking.

A few examples to have an idea about the public system, in general. This is where she is going to work, and she feels very happy about it. She finally managed it.

She is making her bed every night and she feels very happy and creative about each new day. She is not bored at all but she is full of energy and passion. She cares about nothing, she thinks about nothing, she hopes about nothing, she steps on both legs upwardly and very steadily. She wants to show off, and she thinks she is somebody, a VIP. Too airy and confident for our system! We have to bring her down to earth somehow, but how?

She has over evaluated herself and instead of having an inferiority complex, she has developed, through her experiences, a superiority complex, being very grateful to the highest spiritual strengths now ruling her life and transforming her into a beautiful, intelligent and most of all modest young lady.

No comments.

If you have any comments send them to our magazine.

Thank you!

**

THE COMEBACK... THE PUBLIC

"The government changed but love remained...," and with the new government policy an air of freedom and modernization blew over the Greek social system, too. According to Law No... Article No... a 5% of handicapped citizens claim the right to be assigned to state institutions and ministries and serve the public as civil servants.

Resurrection! Joy to the world!

Finally, we joined the rest of the world. Five per cent of all state employees who happen to be "handicapped" would get a permanent post in the public and be so grateful to the new minister who had established so prosperous and graceful laws to protect the human rights of some minorities. A great favor! To throw at last a bone to the hungry mongrels.

Joy to the people living behind the Iron Curtain of the state establishment!

Joy to the underground people of the most precious country in the world!

Then, we, the invalids started to rush forth to get information in order to submit our applications for an appointment in public service. Longing for a place under our brilliant sun... We were no longer obliged to pass through elementary, secondary, and advanced committees of brain-washed scientists deciding about our life and future. Treated even worse than the communists of that time who were being pursued like demons by the military government of their own people! Another condition of applying to public service for employment during those harsh times was the famous "Certificate of Political Conviction," otherwise you were excluded forever from a broad array of social affairs and institutional opportunities.

Free from the procedural torture that had so recently prevailed, I too submitted my application while my career was drawing to a close in that town where the small school was prospering and becoming famous for its uniqueness! A lot of students and a lot of money. My golden years! Yes, indeed. Hard work and personal values raised me to the top. I had proved, first to myself and then to the others, that I wasn't at all useless and invalid.

I may have boasted but I had never compromised my initial principles.

Now I am standing face to face with Selfie again. I look at my photo...

There is a battle again between us. Although I became a successful businesswoman, I was still yearning for a post in the public school. What nonsense! To abandon everything, a seven-year project and apply for a poorly-paid job at a public school! Isn't that crazy?! One part of myself was advising me to stay there and go on with my prosperous business and the other one was pushing me violently ahead for a job in public service.

Why...?

Just only to prove that I could finally work in the public school along with the "normal" people. Or maybe it was just because I had been working very hard in my private school and I needed less working hours? Proof of my capability, normality...?

"Bearing witness to the real love for that school; how am I going to abandon it?"

It was, definitely, the first reason that forced me to that final decision. To abandon everything I had created all those years without any help — particularly from my own country, my own people — and start again from the beginning in a new post, which in the past was a "restricted area" for me; absolutely forbidden! Banned from the field of competition! Besides exhaustion and hardship, I think that was the main reason I applied to the public school system.

I only wish to vent my frustration on the new world now opened up to me after so many years where I had been mercilessly rejected many years ago. It was a difficult task to escape my prejudice, that's why I could not think reasonably. Those inhibitions! How much they can affect you. They force you to function unreasonably, mostly biased.

Allied to that final decision to serve in the public school system were additional, albeit minor, factors. The first of these subordinate reasons was the social environment of a secluded small town, having nothing besides nature and relaxation to offer to its people; this was not the best choice for a young energetic and ambitious woman. Add to this the fact that life there was under tight scrutiny of influential locals, forever inspected by the merciless community driven by humble intellectual standards of sophistication that were intimately wedded to extremely conservative and old-fashioned social and political perspectives. No revolution had ever begun in a place like that. Flat people, flat thinking, all of which has an effect on a dynamic mind not unlike a big marsh lying among their houses that was incrementally drained for the sake of their historical cultivations. Well-off, but poor mentally and spiritually; without any prospective, without hope...

The second reason was too much work. From the morning on till late at night. Too many responsibilities concerning teachers, parents, students, the running of a good business, training seminars and education at the same time.

The third reason was the prospect of a momentous change! Something different, something else, a new era!

I gave up money for a better life. That is still my motto, anyway. The quality and not the quantity of life matters!

It took me exactly four years since that day to get my appointment to the state educational system. It wasn't too late, just in time to take a big breath and turn a new page. The procedure of selling my small school had already started; in the meantime I had to go on managing its operation otherwise all the students would have departed. I was mad, out of my mind, to leave almost four hundred students and climb the wild mountains of Crete.

"You have to pass through that door, too, do you hear me? Don't stay on the threshold only!"

"Yes, Selfie, yes."

My first school was in Crete, Kritsa, twenty kilometers outside of Agios Nikolaos city. It was a big village in a mountainous area where a junior high school of one hundred pupils was operating. Before I could take up my new post, I had to prepare my small school for the new students' registrations. The right time, the right moment! I just could not sell the business like that, in a light consciousness and just leave, I had to make the necessary preparations for the next "heir to the throne" — the next boss. Crete was so far away for me to serve as a teacher and at the same time care for the private school until it would be sold. There must be a solution, I had to do something.

During that time, my brother, a teacher too, was working at a public school in downtown Athens. One of his colleagues was an important member of the PA.SO.K[4] political party. This colleague was also a vice-president in the teacher's union. Most of such position-holders work as institutional "go-betweens" and deal brokers while also gauging the landscape for strategic electoral support. These practices, unfortunately, have come to constitute a bad tradition that results in a problematic mutuality between the people and the politicians; vote-seekers looking for victims whom they benefit from while providing little public advocacy. Such positions are prized and permanent posts after a long service in the public sector! Such political corruption is the particularly prominent reason for the rapid decline of Greek civil life.

Corruption and charity go together. For me it was charity.

"Why don't you tell your friend Yiannis to support my assignment at a school post in Athens so that I can look after my business, too?" I asked my brother, hoping to benefit from his connection.

---

[4] Initials standing for the Panhellenic Socialistic Movement

"He is not my friend, and I don't know him very well."

"Get to know him and tell him you voted for PA.SO.K. You belong to that political party and you have a handicapped sister who wants to be in Athens because she requires specialized medical treatment. I can supply you with the necessary doctor's certifications."

"I hate those guys. I don't want any favors from them," he said doggedly.

"Come on, tell him that our whole family is going to vote for his party. He is new in the political game and he may help me. Please!"

"Why didn't you stay at your splendid private school? Now you want to be appointed to a public one? I just can't understand. What kind of perversion is that?" He was so damn right.

"We'll talk about it another time. Now I need your help. You don't have anything to lose."

"My peace!"

"How so?"

"Then, I would be obliged to go to their union meetings, you see! He would compel me to take part in things I hate..."

"It's up to you to keep up the balances. Only think, that if I go to Crete, I will lose my school and the money, of course. At least till I sell it."

Relenting, Jacob sighed. "Ok, I'll see what I can do."

I went by *Minoan Lines* to Crete and registered as a teacher in my new school and gave the usual oath of the civil servant. What a fake! I'd already started making use of my handicap to draw the attention — pity or mercy — of the people in keeping with the school principals, since I needed some time off to prepare the registrations of the students in my own small school. Besides, I had to prepare myself for the next great step; that was to get a school posting in Athens. An important reason was my handicap. I had learned very fast to adjust and convert my disadvantage into an advantage for my own profit and welfare.

The injections had been in fact very effective!

While sailing back to Piraeus in board *Minoan Lines'* ship *Aretousa*, I am enjoying the morning wind and recalling the recent facts. Crete was a beautiful island; it would have been a very nice place for my first appointment in public education. However my existing job was still very important to me. Nevertheless, I couldn't keep it, for it was illegal for a civil servant to simultaneously run a business. I had to sell it by any means. I was committed to serving the public school system as a civil servant.

"It is about a public education offered freely to citizens..."

I was pressing my brother like hell to speak to that Union guy about me. I clung to him like a bee on honey, and I would not relent till he finally said yes. I was right because the guy "became a carpet to be stepped on," which means he became remarkably willing to help me through my brother even though he had never met me. The fact is that he sent me right away to the Secretary of the Minister of Education and everything worked out fast and perfect just the way I wanted.

My assignment to a school in Athens came a few days later and here I was serving as a teacher in the 15th High School in Kipseli. The headmaster from the school in Crete couldn't believe his ears when informed of my assignment. He thought I was very well connected with influential politicians, and since that day, as a prominent executive of the political party PA.SO.K., he passed the rumor that a teacher (me) had given her oath in his school but she had never kept it.

I managed to keep my own private school rolling on, dedicating more and more time to the procedure of selling it.

After school, three times a week, I drove 130 km each way from Athens to my private school to assist in instruction and reassure parents and kids that I had not abandoned them. The rumors of my appointment at the public school in Athens had already spread around the small community. I become so sad when I think of it now, as they loved and respected me, and feared losing me. However I "had" to turn that new page... an inner necessity... There I had been "cured" of sorts. But now I had to proceed further to the next station of my life.

At last, after a full year of commuting back and forth in my car in the dark of night, my private school was sold. It was purchased by a teacher of Italian who wore a scarf on her head called Julia. After my departure most of the students left, compelling Julia to shut down the school of some 380 students. The very thought of it is still a source of great irritation for me.

Another circle was completed and now I moved to draw the next one!

ATHENS PUBLIC SCHOOLS

The Greek public sector, for those who have no idea how this fantastic service works, is an equally dreary and piteous story.

The unhappiness of being a Greek civil servant! Misery and apathy, conservatism and imitativeness, cheating and idleness in all its majestic manifestations. Especially for someone coming from a freelance profession, the public sector seemed like a disaster that descended upon us from some alien planet. Surviving it is contingent to adjusting to clichés, narrow-mindedness and vacant performance. People working at public posts never become fighters...

I was one of those who supported "public reform," thus, all the principals had a great problem with me. They were immensely averse towards the taking on of any responsibilities beyond the narrowest sphere of responsibility and they entirely lacked initiative; these environs was inhabited by very small and inadequate people covering their unimportant existence behind an authoritative post. At times they were asked to make decisions about our comprehensive future in the public school system; something they were entirely inadequate to do. In the past they functioned as spies of the system, ensuring stagnation and stasis. During the Junta they cooperated with the inspectors of the Ministry of Education in the exact same capacity. Leftists and willful teachers were routinely threatened with an adverse and unfavorable appointment to a village in the obscure periphery of the country. Most instructors were unprepared and overwhelmed by the demands of the posts that they held, challenging them on a daily basis with the thousands of problems routinely encountered in the big public schools of Athens. They dreaded the thought of losing that prominent post in the public school due to their inability to offer anything in the classroom or had been born with the expectation of a person who simply "gave orders." Besides that, there was a small bonus in addition to the salary.

Thank God, it was their problem and not mine.

From the outset I was positioned as their enemy. Only a few of them accepted me the way I was; those became my friends. This was particularly the case at my first school in Athens. It was a very big school with middle class pupils, well balanced and organized because the principal was very capable. Strict and fair! Mr. Apostolou!

In the beginning he could not accept my insubordinate and rebellious personality, but as time passed he started appreciating and respecting me for what I was. He had been watching me functioning as a teacher and as a person; that is the reason he finally warmed to my disposition in the end. At a farewell birthday party commemorating his forty years of service and fully pensioned retirement, he told me in front of all the thirty five teachers.

"Never change, never give up, go ahead like that, you became a good symbol for your students and for us, too. We've all learned from you here... Watch out for the traps, though, my dear Zavolia..."

In contrast, another principal called me an "autistic and guttersnipe" in front of all the teachers. I remained for some people "a person with special needs," "retarded," mentally and physically because I could not fit into conventional patterns and forms.

In ever adjusted to the civil service environment anyway; never felt a part of the social status we were generally accredited with. I was a social outcast and general misfit because of those poorly-concealed sentiments. It was a confirmation of reality, for the fact was that I "was" different from others.

Why should I fit somewhere? Why should I belong somewhere? I even refused membership in the Union of Handicapped People.

I only wished to do my job and earn my living. I wished to work a few hours and have enough free time for my hobbies and leisure. I had become strong and dense, as durable as a rock. Even if they kicked me out of the public school system, I was so sure I would start my life anew without missing a step. I had already tried it, and I had been successful.

"Go further and always ahead...!"

My life had been through "fire and iron" and no obstacle get in my way. In the school I tried to be formal but not ceremonial. For the time being, I took refreshing breaths of vigor from those fantastic kids. The youth...!

My own youth...! That's why I understood their way of thinking.

Those splendid and wonderful kids — "my kids" — made beautiful what was the cold, impersonal, ugly and suffocating place of the public school. Most of the public schools are similar to those multi-blocked high-rises of the former east European communist countries that housed thousands of families.

The kids made those ugly buildings vibrate with energy and youth. At times, of course they forced us teachers to resort to tranquillizers in order to recover from managing them. But the schools were "regenerated" by the most vivid and rare colors of youthful existence. Our students in my eyes looked like war aircrafts, phantoms, tearing up the horizons, which either made you deaf with their noise or they put you by force next to the cock pit and let you fly unwillingly with them. The flight was fascinating.

Something is happening with those young people, something is happening. Something unique is happening — superb, which very few of the teachers realize; those that do have a good time with those rebels, the rest who don't see cannot contextualize their rejection by the student's community.

Beyond those kids there is nothing else for the uninspired instructor but despair, misery and chaos.

Sunk into despair on the one hand and optimism on the other hand, I managed to survive in that neurotic environment. I invested my whole energy and knowledge in those young people, our students and I neglected most of my colleagues whether they be young, middle-aged or old since they were "a burnt playing card." In my heart though I've kept some names I would never forget, Mary, the French teacher, Tassia, the math teacher, Giorgos and Spyros teaching ancient and modern Greek, Alex, the PE teacher and coach of the school's basketball team.

Most important was the benefit of the immediate awareness of my social positioning. I was not a freelance business woman any more but a civil servant belonging to the working class with rights and restrictions I had to face. That was a very good lesson I learned very well in our union meetings, but I once again refused to join and serve the union for apparent reasons. That was another chapter for me. I had been following the proceedings of the union closely, taking part on rare occasion, and voting casually when convenient despite being proselytized to attend their parties. Now, when I look back, I see most of the famous names of our union leaders at the top of the political life in my country. Thank God, I stayed away from all that corruption!

"The knowledge and the experience of the guards," like a Greek proverb says.

Now living again in Athens in the social center of Greek life, I liked "Selfie" very much. Outside of Athens nothing happens. The province and the country are for the pensioners and the retired from life, for the "unthinkable and retarded" as well. I wished no return… to the native land!

Then I took my long tongue out and I started licking like hell. I knocked on all the doors I knew, longing like a mongrel for "a piece of bread" under the magic name. A permanent post at the schools in Athens, transferred from Crete where I was first assigned.

I had worked in both beautiful and ugly schools with great teachers and "small" teachers who were moving back and forth without noticing anything of the big miracles that were arrayed all around us in the school. These miracles seemingly elicited no effect upon their disposition, as if they were simply the droning repetition of stock images passing in front of their eyes without penetrating deeper.

Only the kids, those fantastic young people, only those were moving, were changing, were marching ahead while still remaining innocent kids.

I overcame the "non-updated" colleagues with great steps and imprinted the miracles on my mind. The teaching hours were sometimes long and arduous but more often they constituted a long interesting pilgrimage to the altar of the classics, to the thinkers, the reformers, a hint and a flame to enter the mythical figures within the innocent eyes of our students just before their miserable and unfair integration into vacuous rituals of social life and the faux emancipations of their postmodern souls into a stagnating society which clings to its traditions out of fear rather than respect.. A gust of fresh wind, those young people, a bottle of oxygen for deep and dangerous dives into the dark blue tranquility of the sea water!

Should someone be prepared and ready for all without waiting for the big joys of the body and the heart? My own strength is my supreme wish to be patient and persistent as well as not allowing a sober memory to interfere with the splendor of the unexpected.

"*The sky is a light, the earth is another light and my horizon is clear and free every time I attempt to take a deep look at it,*" the verses of our great poet, Giorgos Seferis, I am recalling.

In that special phase of my life, I felt so free to look at the long horizons expecting something unexpected however still expecting the conventional. It is always like that just before a sudden tornado will overcome you. I feel the winds beginning to swirl, a weird intuition The whole I is preparing without my conscious consent... unconsulted as to timing... it will come. It is on the way. I can almost touch it...

On a practical basis, I was free and beautiful, independent, living alone in a cozy apartment in Maroussi, a suburb of Athens. The suburb had been manipulated aesthetically by its high-income residents and glory-seekers, mayors, etc. I had friends from the past and friends of the present, all hoping to be friends of the future. I was going out with some very special colleagues whose views and way of life diverged from those often considered "normal." The normal system; if there is normality in the system, ever!

They were often present but rarely in attendance, travelers of the souls, both untouchables and illuminators, artists, mysticists, philosophers. We had all jumped out of our bodies and we had been desperately searching a convergence of souls to be joined by a touch, a glimpse of an eye, a half-erased note, a melody, a fine taste of the palette. We had coordinated and united old and new friends into a long simmering twilight of desires and passions, in a perplexing network of the senses.

It was as though I had been paralyzed and all of a sudden I started to walk. As though I had fallen into a deep lethargy before being pinched to consciousness by those who thought I might have died.

Better is to genuinely sleep than live in a state of slumber. The liberty I had conquered hurt me so much exactly like the bondage that had deprived me of my oxygen.

My priorities for the time were traveling to the open skies.

I was looking ahead... my wish to make another big journey in life... *"The oil here is burning fast; that night will be cold in the eternity..."*

To change my life again, take another course — but how?

The people who had walked into my life at this stage had not lasted long. I kept the souls who suited my taste and mood as a convenient stock of social sustenance to be tapped when needed. The parameters of the relationships were delimited from the beginning, and each bore an expiration date. Every seven or ten years, a fascinating event jolted me from the monotony of daily life, cheating whirls and wisps of potential change in a variety of colors.

I slowly stepped into the full maturity of my adulthood — a point "just" prior to the acceptance of middle-age. I was living a mellow life full of conventional experiences and indifferent passions. Intangible, indefinite!

The stoic passing of time which slowly coarsened the skin as well as our soul! Surviving on an endless hope for a distinctive tomorrow.

What? Exactly like now, even though you are carrying many more years on your shoulders. To those who denigrate the art of hoping, there is no hope; sentiments reflected in the lives of many people of similar circumstances to myself. With such people, I sometimes resonate, wondering whether that is the sign that I require another supporting or restorative injection! Perhaps a big dose...

I thought I had "consumed" all the kinds of injections. The swelling in my buttocks was gone and now fresh, new, white and tempting were seeking the big dose...

"I need desperately my dose," as we say!

In fact, speaking of "doses," the next one arrived by plane next summer!

A hot sultry summer!

ANDRE, THE GERMAN TIGER

Phoenikouda or "Taverna," as it is usually called by the locals, is a small fishing village at the west edge of the Peloponnese. It is sheltered in quiet obscurity in the Messenian Gulf, faint but brighter than the sun, overshadowed by the petty indulgences of avarice, drink, and frivolity and whatever satisfies our hearts.

Amen!

Both short and long summers I have taken to spending there with my good friends who offered me their hospitality.

Anemomylos in Greek or "windmill" in English, still exists as a camping site on an exotic white sand beach that stretches a hundred kilometers. It happened to be the property of my best friend's husband and his family who came from that village. All of them Phoenikouda dwellers...

So simple and beautiful it was, born of the first harnessing of mother nature from which it acquired its name from the Phoenician merchants and explorers who were the first recorded colonists of the site.

To be living in a small tent under the canopy of saline trees, enjoying the rising and setting of the sun, the sea and the sand.

The tent was a present from my mountainous cousins in America. It was my principal possession along with a big appetite for life and adventure. Then...

Needless to say that companies and companies of friends and strangers were getting together on the coast, by the waves, under the moon, easy going, spontaneous and primitive, without racism and class struggle. Simply like that. Our best friend was the tempting, challenging, provoking and fascinating Greek summer.

Phoenikouda lies on the coast, spreading its legs into the sea water, as if licking its feet. Having little consciousness of its perception by others, the small village had no idea how to retain its beauty and keep it secretly sealed and pure. But somehow the elegant simplicity of the site had survived. But the base elements of the sun and sea cannot be easily purloined by anybody, besides the witches, that is!

Phoenikouda was totally transformed when I saw it after many years. Still picturesque but deprived of the colors and that fine evergreen aroma of the past. New architecture and holiday styling, there had been a dire transmutation just to fit more foreign visitors, signs, and adventurous invaders! Nevertheless, it was my last shelter and harbor after summer holidays in August just before the beginning of the school year the following month.

Summer nights are magical even though you have not enough money or you are not in love, since you are enamored at the most elemental level with the natural immediacy of the surroundings. Traps are set everywhere...

One special night our gathering had almost finished dinner in an atmosphere that was not the best in light of some small arguments which had altered the mood. So I was the first to say good night and leave the group.

I went straight to the bar to put a half-full bottle of wine in the fridge.

I banged the bottle at the bar shield and ordered the barman to put it in the fridge.

"You are going to break it, you don't have to pump it so hard on the wood," I heard somebody telling me in English.

"Why do you care about it? Why don't you mind your own business?" I said to him rudely in English again.

In a distinct apologetic tone, he said, "Sorry, I was only joking."

I looked at him angrily and I moved to the exit with my customary limp. In trying to negotiate a small stair which separated the bar from the restaurant, I took a tremendous fall. My good leg was twisted so strongly I thought I had broken it. I tried to get up but I could not move for the pain. I may have screamed too because all of a sudden a paper tiger is springing towards me and a man is kneeling down at my side. He supports me as I rise to my feet. It is impossible for me to walk. In the meantime everybody has gathered trying curiously to find out what has happened.

"Do you want me to help you sit somewhere?" the tiger man is asking me politely. At the very moment I turned my head I realized it was the same guy who had been sitting at the bar. Even though in terrible pain, I felt so ashamed of my reflexively aggressive response to his comment at the bar.

"No, thanks, I would like to go to my tent but I don't think I can walk," I told him. "It hurts like hell."

"Would you allow me to help you?" he enquired again.

"Of course," I say, trying to be polite.

Then the big tiger is taking me up in his arms and is carrying me to my tent. Onlookers followed us, for it was a spectacle of sorts. There, out of the tent, he puts me smoothly on a small bed and is kneeling in front of me, testing my foot to see if I can move it or no. The pain is unbearable.

"I think I've broken it. I'm in terrible pain."

"We can take you to the hospital in Kalamata," my friends state.

Rather gallantly, the paper tiger states: "It's not broken."

"How do you know? Are you a doctor or something?" I said with equal measures of petulance and disregard.

"I am a poor cop. No doctor. But I know everything about first aid and signs of fractures. You've stumbled and twisted your ankle. That's it! Trust me!" he said looking straight into my eyes.

"I am going to get you something from my car and by tomorrow it will be all right."

The guileless simplicity of his eyes elicited an immediate confidence and consent.

He returned momentarily with cream and a bandage. He spread the cream over my ankle, massaged it a bit, then wrapped and secured the bandage carefully over my entire foot.

"Tomorrow it will be better," he smiled with assurance.

"Thank you, thank you very much for everything... and I really apologize for my behavior."

"I don't recall a thing," he said gallantly. "And it's my duty to help people."

"Are you an American cop?"

"No, I am German, a Berliner."

"Really? What are you doing here?" I insisted despite the shooting pain in my ankle. The throbbing distraction did not preclude me from noting how good looking he was, and appreciating the quality of his sympathy.

"I am on holiday. I've been visiting this place for about eight years."

"Really? How come we have never met? I've been on holidays for years here myself."

"Well, we met now. It happened now," he said while patting my leg.

He had a very sweet smile and supple brown eyes that looked particular large due to his long eye lashes. He was well-tanned and had a thick moustache. His whole look was not that of a German but of a Mediterranean guy, perhaps from Crete.

"I thought all Germans were blond," I commented with a smile.

"Not all."

Referring to his medical skills, I asked, "How is it that you know all those things?"

"I have attended special seminars at police school about first aid. I know a lot. When the policemen in our unit get injured, I give them first aid. All of us in our unit know how to give first aid to people or each other. That's a part of our training and education."

"Very interesting. You've been my guardian angel tonight. Otherwise I might have had to go to the hospital."

"I have to go now. I am very tired. I will drop in tomorrow to see how you are doing. What's your name by the way?"

"Zavolia or Aglaopi, that's how my grandmother called me."

"Geez, both of them are difficult," he stated with amusement.

"Don't you have an easier one?"

"No, I'm sorry, call me 'pssst,' 'pssst,' like the pussy cats."

"I think the first one is easier. Z-a-v-o-l-i-a, right?"

"Yes, that's right," I said, hopefully concealing that he had already struck my fancy.

"Tell me again the other one."

With great deliberation, I spelled the Greek name out: "A-g-l-a-o-p-i."

"Who is she? That is a peculiar name. Both of them sound rather strange to me. Maybe because I do not speak Greek very fluently."

"Well, you will learn. I'm a teacher. I can teach you. The first name means a person who is constantly causing small problems and the other one is a siren from Greek mythology — a bird with a head of a beautiful woman. There were three or five of these sirens who fascinated the sailors with their melodic voice, compelling them to sail no further. Instead, the sailors remained on that island and could not move from it. While sailing along that island, Odysseus ordered his men to tie him on the mast while he put wax in his ears so that he would not hear their seductive melodies."

"Well, very interesting story. Is that your own way to enchant people?" he asked with a petulant persistence.

"I don't think I can manage quite so well."

"You may think so, but ask other people what they think about it."

I felt something peculiar then.

He stood up and gave me his hand so as to excuse himself for the night.

My good friend Maria intuitively stepped forth. "Why don't you come tomorrow morning for a good Greek breakfast?"

"With pleasure for the breakfast, but I'll come any way to see how our lady is doing," he said gesturing towards me. "What time?"

"Ten, eleven, whenever you wake up," Maria said.

"All right, I have to go now. I am very tired. Get well and good night." He waved his hand and left. The turn of his gaze left his body exposed to our uncensored scrutiny. What a gorgeous body.

"What a guy!" Maria exclaimed.

"What a guy!" I echoed.

"What do you think?" Maria asked.

"I don't know anything yet," I said. "Not quite yet."

Next morning I felt better but I still could not walk. So Maria prepared breakfast and it was almost eleven when we saw Andre coming.

"I apologize for being late but I overslept."

"Take your time, you are on holiday," Maria said.

I was lying on a small bed out of the tent as he approached.

"How is your leg today?"

"It's much better but I still can't walk. When I put weight on it, it hurts."

"Let's go swimming then, after breakfast," he said exuberantly.

"I don't think I'll make it."

"Of course you will, I'll take you on with my arms like last night. Didn't you like it?"

"Oh, thank you it was very nice of you last night, but I don't think I want to go to the sea like that."

"I'll take care of you, don't worry. I'm a strong man," he said playfully.

I did not reflect his casual disposition. "I'd rather stay here today."

"All right, all right, I was kidding, if you don't feel like it, it's fine. Another day, when you get well." He deflected the discord by turning to Maria.

"Well, well, you have nice stuff here for breakfast."

They sat next to me and we had breakfast together. He was not only a fantastic guy to look, but a good conversationalist, too. In addition to his duties as a policeman in Berlin, he referenced the "Wall of Shame," his world travels, his beloved motorcycle that he periodically raced, his divorced parents, fantastic mother, and a brother that had died young. This has been the first time he had come to Greece alone, an unexpected occurrence in light of a fight with his girlfriend that compelled her to cancel the trip.

"I think it was fatal to meet you," he said, looking first to me and then at Maria.

Thank God that my friend Maria was married or I might have been jealous. He spoke perfect English and in my question about this facility, he said he had studied at an American school in Afghanistan while his father was assigned as a teacher at a technical school. He seemed so simple, so warm-hearted — though a German, his disposition and appeal was much more like I might associated with a Greek. He helped prepare the breakfast and then they jointly cleared the table. Having a bike, he offered to do the daily shopping for us. We all had a very good time together and when he got up to leave, it was past midday.

"Well I'm going to dive for a while and afterwards sit under the sun for a stretch."

"You mean under the umbrella?"

"No, definitely not. I'm not using an umbrella. I want to enjoy the sun. That's rare in Germany, and my German cold body misses it. I want to store the whole sun of Greece into my heart; its bright way of life and warmth."

"You have both enough," Maria said to him.

"You think so..?" he enquired.

"Yes. Positively."

"Well I'm glad you have that impression of me," he said with a graceful smile.

Andre left, promising to swing by later or the following day.

"Gosh, he's a tiger," exclaimed Maria. "It's a pity I'm married. Look lively. Why are you lying there and you didn't let him take you to the sea?"

"I don't know him yet."

"I think he is very fond of you. He clearly fancies you."

"How do you know?"

"That stands out a mile. He seems to be a nice guy. My instincts never deceive me."

"Well, time will tell. Besides, best put a check on any interest I might have. He is good looking indeed but don't forget — he is a German."

"And so what about him being a German?" she asked angrily.

"I don't know."

My words were not far from reality. I had not fallen for him, but Maria had already given voice to a little voice of infatuation deep down in my mind that would not abide by my skepticism.

Andre began to visit my camp regularly. My leg was getting better every day, allowing me to overcome my initial hesitation and go swimming with him. He was a championship swimmer and always assisted me when I returned to the beach. He was kind and careful. I had never before met such a man in my life. He was something different from the Greek model of masculinity, being exceptional in everything. The men I had met besides Georgis were profoundly selfish and laden with complexes tethered to their narcissism. Other men liked me as a woman but qualified me as a "special case" of sorts. It was never spoken aloud, but I knew it. I had felt it. I think they would have liked me if I were normal, as one of them did say to me once in an unguarded moment.

It was Tassos, the fellow from Pontos who wanted to invest in me, offering another transatlantic trip to America to have an operation and become normal, like the rest. I refused, stating that "I liked me very much the way I was." I was not interested at all in visiting America again. I was in peace and harmony with myself now. He was staring at me as though I was a peculiar species, a UFO, an alien. He couldn't say a word afterwards his "generous" offer was rejected. Thank God, I did not marry him because all of my fantastic injections would have been in vain.

Andre was such an exceptional guy. He seemed to have no complexes at all. He was easy-going and treated me like the sole woman of beauty in an often hideous and unjust world. I had a crazy desire to fall in love with him. He had a fantastic sense of humor, was a good speaker, laconic but pleasant. He liked teasing people to lend a measure of humor and whimsy to their life; although his commitment to the act often caused us to presume he meant everything he said. An innocent soul in a grown man's body; well-built as well. An "Aegean body" my friend Maria used to say.

Then, finally, he invited me for dinner, just me — only me. There was a full moon that night. And what a night! I chose a very idyllic and traditional small tavern on a hill where the full moon could be seen in its entity. Under the grape-laden pergola the tables were overlain with checkered tablecloths and surrounded by hundreds of earthen pots with seasonal flowers. Fantastic environment and delicious food! Our veins seemed to flow with wine and anticipation.

He held my hand from the very outset of our walk, and never let it go the entire extent of our stroll. "I fell in love with you from the very beginning," he said with a casual sincerity that I found elegant in its simplicity. "From the moment I saw you and took you in my arms. I don't know if that is prudent but it is certainly real and honest. This is how I feel. I cannot change it. I would like to marry you and take you to Berlin with me."

"What?" I asked with undisguised shock.

"You heard what I had to say!" he said with a distinct undercurrent of gravity.

"But you don't know me and I don't know you at all!" I exclaimed.

"You'll get to know me… provided you want to, of course."

The August moon made night look like day, and seemed to render us speechless at times as we ate dinner and quietly sipped wine.

The twilight of the Gods!

The daylight of the people!

The horizon was disrupted by the profile of Schiza, a small island opposite the land. The sea was tranquil, like a mirror reflecting shimmering streams of the moon's light directly upon us. A full round moon inviting us to a mystic dance of our senses! The moon was dripping love...

What kind of God was playing with our passions? A deep silence scattered all over, a devout pilgrimage to the altar of Celestine.

Enchanted by the moon, indeed, the evening was magical.

"I want to take you with me to Berlin. I love you and I don't want to leave you behind. I want to marry you," he said once again.

"For sure, a crazy priest must have baptized him... What nonsense he is talking about...."

"You hardly know me and you want to marry me?" I asked in wonderment.

"I've just heard your heart beats and short breath; that's why I've understood everything." He simply said, smiling at me.

"You haven't understood anything. Time makes miracles that announce themselves," I told him cryptically.

"Do you mean that time erodes the miracle?

"That, too!"

"Then, why don't we just let time do as it will?" He asked.

"It should be like that, I suppose," I responded.

"There is no 'should' and 'must.' When the soul speaks, time comes second."

"Do you think so?"

"It is so," he asserted.

When I woke up the next morning, I looked at the day with completely different eyes.

Fatal was that evening! The real meaning of his words, so spontaneously conveyed, did not affect me dramatically at that particularly time. Yet, it was a foreshadowing union of two people. A fatal meeting of two souls!

Before the evening came to an end, I announced to him that I had to return to school in Athens on the 1st of September. Despite having fifteen days remaining on his vacation, he said he would leave Phoenikouda too because staying without me was hurtful to him.

"I'll come back though in two months," he stated. "Assuming that you want me too?"

In two months he was back. Our love was transcendental, suspended at the limits of our passions, seemingly at the point where the elemental experience of humanity naturally intertwined with the infinite. Both my eyes and my soul were replete with his presence. They could not store other expectations. They could not store other promises. That love had to pay its homage to the time coming after us.

He called two or three times during daylight hours to tell me "I love you," to be followed by more calls at night when the telephone costs were cheaper.

He spelled out unspoken words. We each gave each other detailed and extensive reports about our thoughts and daily activities over the phone.

He wrote me a letter every day, letters which sometimes arrived bundled together in the post. Familiar with the significance of such bundled correspondence, the postman shared a conspiratorial smile with me as I anticipated his deliveries. Letters full of passionate words and feelings immersed deeply in honeyed prose, scattered photos and small tokens of our time spent together.

"I want you to come with me to Berlin," he said. "I would be so distressed to leave you back again! I can't bear it anymore," he said as soon as he got off the plane with a big bouquet of beautiful colored flowers and fell into my arms. He held me so tight I couldn't breathe.

"These are for you; fresh flowers from the blossomed gardens of Holland," he whispered in my ears while still holding me in his arms.

Later on at home he opened his suitcase. He had brought me small and big packages. His gifts.

Andre impressed me tremendously, that northern European fellow of Aryan descent. From which planet had he come from? Was it a God or a devil that sent him? Was he real? I pinched him to assure myself that I was not dreaming.

"Eh, you're hurting me," he uttered, before freeing easing myself away from him. With a measure of humorous incredulity I stated.

"I want to find out whether you are real or not."

Indeed he seemed to be real. Human flesh full of life and health! Alive, vivid, outgoing and warm. A constant surprise being with him! An exotic adventure!

Nothing was spent or consumed unreasonably. Eternal love it seemed to be! Suddenly we had developed an appetite for the intense immediacy of sensations that had always been at hand. The fire was not far away, we could smell the smoke and we started feeling its flame sealing our hearts. I guided him all around to the beauties of my country, my most beloved places he had only seen up to that point through the eyes of a common tourist. I lent him my eyes to see what he had already seen but in fact he had never seen. I took him a tour of my country up to its distant edge, beyond the surface he was familiar with to its very depths.

Impulsive, warm, communicative! Not at all selfish. An endless Thanksgiving, his love... No effort to compete with a rival, only the acknowledgment of a friend, a lover. Incredibly attractive and sincerely fascinating — two sentiments that must be counted amongst the most generous of spirits! He was the one, the incomparable one for me! He was the one that comes only once in life... and never again.

The perception of time was obliterated by plenitude. It conveyed his sentiments. Time has become its servant and it bows in front of him.

Who else? Passion arrests time; it is why all humans at one point or another offer themselves on the altar of love.

In the beginning, I could not believe it. I thought I was dreaming, living an illusion, lying under the effect of a very strong narcotic. Looking however for the lost time I had consumed searching deep inside to discover me. I had been through various relationships but for me males were a means to an end. I enjoyed them but only in small portions, and those were never enough to satisfy a much more profound hunger. They lacked the critical spice which gave a much more definitive flavor to life that I desired.

Seeking for the best, the perfect, the soft-focused dream I had envisioned and thought was achievable. None of the men that I had known was enough for my taste, compelling me at times to forego the hope that he would come.

He came five minutes before the expiration date... All good things come when you have given up hope of their arrival. In my personal life good things happened "two minutes to..." It's easy to say that life still owes me something, like a credit...

Perhaps Andre was kind of a reward. A priceless compensation for the great injustice that accented every step I took.

The fulfillment of time.

The last hope and the highest ideal!

A metaphysical transcendence.

However, when the apparent limits of the transcendent, the exceptional, are themselves exceeded, Gods become very angry, inciting them to hurl incendiaries of an entire different sort down upon the earth on the earth and its inhabitants.

How come Gods can behave arrogantly and proudly and people cannot?

How come they can decide on our fortunes and adversities while we cannot?

Well, I have made up my mind to take control of my own adventure in happiness and care not about their caprices. There is no reasonable explanation but only a metaphysical logic since in the near future there was nothing left.

We come into the world with a clear mandate to be cast out of it one day; therefore we must — by any means possible — summon the fortitude to survive and be prepared for a pending departure whose timing is vague.

Creativity is the code, the PIN, the password!

I still feel that life has left me an open line credit... So why do I have the sense of inadequacy that is native to mortality? Is that ungratefulness? Should I keep my mouth shut instead?

Andre came into my life to compensate for an old forgotten debt; the burden of existence that had been my own life. However though the bounty of sensation he brought created another debt — a debt that was impossible to be repaid, even in a hundred years.

Games of Fate; never anticipated!

That is to pay a fine for joy and happiness. Unpaid bills have to be paid otherwise they become a noose around the throat. Most of the bills are settled, sooner or later. Everything has its price and its own peculiar honor. All of us will pay for our delights one day, some at a higher rate than others.

It was during his fifth visit in five months to Greece that Andre told me: "Our relationship has become rather expensive." It happened to be my birthday.

"Am I so expensive for you?" I was teasing him.

"I think so. You've become too expensive and I can't afford you as you are. So pack your things and hurry up and join me in Berlin. The sooner the better," he coyly stated.

"I'll come in April."

His face took on a sober tone: "I mean forever!"

"Do you have enough sun in Berlin?"

"Of course we have sun — but maybe not too bright for your Mediterranean taste. It shines for us too, sometimes..."

"I am afraid of the North."

"You have a southern mentality. Not exactly welcoming of a little challenge or adversity. Yet I think it would be the perfect combination: the flame melting the ice."

"Is that so?"

"It will be so," he said reassuringly.

This is how we came to our wedding day, one warm spring night in the rooms of the Mayor's house with our closest friends greeting us with rice and roses in our rose garden like cheerleaders celebrating a win. The event was modest in size and ceremony, not extravagant and ostentatious, no gift registries with graduated price lists as we are accustomed to in Greece!

This is how we formally joined the world and commemorated our union in front of the indiscernible Gods to which we gave the oath of life.

"...till death do us part..."

We gave an oath but life itself cheated us breaking that oath. It coveted our happiness and envied our youth. Better to be envied than pitied...

A NEW HOME TOWN

Against all odds, I fell in love with Germany through Andre's heart.

How could have I denied it? In the beginning, the abrupt integration into an alien place and society was unappealing. And it resulted in Germany having to pay for my bad mood, for my superstitions, for the unbearable weather.

I was denying my husband's country so often the way Peter, one of Jesus Christ's students had disavowed for the same reasons. I was grumbling and cursing reflexively, and refused whatever German thing did not immediately appeal to me. However "Germany fell in love with me" like a woman, at first sight and consequently it did its best to win my affection. She revealed its best colors and pictures little by little to calm my anger down and help to my integration. At the end she covered me with her soft veil till I fell asleep and almost in love with her.

In the beginning I was trying desperately to import my own nationalistic "wishes and musts" into Andre's life, but I failed, and soon relented. He was trying the same way but not so persistently like me; although his approach was ever more graceful than my own! Nevertheless, he failed as well.

Our mutual failure resulted in us falling more deeply in love the way we were against a backdrop multicultural society of dramatic contrasts in skin color, language, and routine sensibilities. We fell in love with what seemed to be a pure, privileged, and mostly inviolable conception of "us" — ignoring the imperfections of what are ultimately insecure and miserable beings thirstily looking for a breath of fresh air.

We reveled in a certain harmony amidst a multicultural society driven by career-driven competition and stress amongst men and women alike.

We lived and enjoyed every single moment. He guided me around Berlin, the West and the East that was dramatically demarcated by the "Wall of Shame." As I had done in Greece, he tried, to show me his country through his own eyes, focusing exactly on the most crucial points of difference between the communist East and the capitalist West; one side defined by its hyper consumption and the other by its palpable inability to do so. The sight of either side did not correspond to its ideological proclamations.

It was so difficult for me to understand such political pageantry constructed out of the crushed and distorted aspirations of the common citizen. In the west there didn't seem to be any security from the majority's power over the minority. It bothered me deeply but afforded this voluntary exile from Greece's imperfections many a good lesson.

Why do all the countries hurt so much…?

I refused even to recognize Germany as a country on the map, negatively standing apart because of the two wars. I was surrounded by an invisible wall prohibiting me to take a look at the other side. Yearning for sun and warmth, Andre soon wanted to revisit Greece. I had long been missing the light and the sun of my brilliant colored country, my friends, and my own people. So many trips together then to Greece were not like his own single trip later on... His life restricting into a short, most impressive sensational and thrilling trip, colorful, richly formed shaping and finely aromatic.

Comforting words quietly uttered from his lips. That special moment is the headline feature of that impressive film.

His work took most of his day. Whatever was left he devoted to his family: "Us" — he and I! He was a conscientious policeman who served the laws of his country obediently and with self-sacrifice at times; the latter was a point of some consternation for me. The jealous Gods always demand sacrifice. Ultimately he sacrificed himself on the altar of his country for the benefit of others, encountering an excess of both corpses and the desiccated souls of the modern city.

A bravery was his own trip! Like heroes marching in the dark!

Left behind, we, the invisible heroes pumping power.

I longed for a long journey again. Time had rolled away so fast... The price of my coming back home was very high!

We went through our seventh and most epicurean year together as I slowly augmented my days with music, art and writing. I was working as a teacher at the Greek High School of Berlin, assigned by our ministry of Education to a five-year term. By then, I had been fully integrated into the German society, I was immersed in the activities and problems of the expatriate Greek community.

We had our small boy, Jacob! Our family!

My happiest years in Berlin were then. Aeolus had opened his sack and all the winds of my country were blowing and I was drifted by its way into the archipelagos to an endless joy and happiness. It was the insane mad nymph who was dancing to the end of love... Although there was no end...

No spare time for hocus-pocus and exorcisms. Somebody had to do something about the gathering storm suspended on the distant horizon.

Who was coming after us? Chasing our lives? Who was jealous of our easy-going selves? Who was standing furtively behind the corner to stab us in the back? I was sensing something weird, peculiar, an approaching evil, but life carried on, there was no time for deep philosophizing. Life had grabbed me from the hair carrying me to its directions. I offered no resistance, enjoying the privileges and joys of indulgence, deeply immersed into a frenzied delirium without end.

Next dawn, there would be no leftovers. We had to move on briskly!

The whole gold of the earth was lying in front my feet! That was the most restoring injection. I had been taking injections without being ill. I was so happy!

I liked them so much! Me crying when I heard the nurse ringing at the door of our house in Athens, preparing to give me an injection. And now, in Berlin, I did not even flinch as my garments dropped to the floor in order to have more injections in my fluffy buttocks! Incredible! What can really happen to somebody! Now I think I was having unlimited doses of a medication of sorts, doses that I really enjoyed. Who knows? I may have always been addicted to all the therapeutic drugs and I hadn't realized.

I needed no more miracles. I seemed to have an abundance of the already circulating in my veins, in my very blood, not simply my dreams. The miracle was I, my own existence. I had overcome my limits. Now I was dreading to know the extent of my capabilities. Maybe I had overestimated my own powers; those hidden ones, deeply sheltered in my broken heart. Look at them! How they came rudely on the surface!? They stick out their tongue, mocking me. I had certainly underestimated them. I had situated them in the most distant margins of my consciousness. Useless, I thought they were.

And now look at them, dancing in front of my eyes, pulsing to the pagan rhythm of the Dionysian communion that was Andre and I.

My sky was light itself, the earth below my feet was a clear and simple backdrop. Bathed in the intense brilliance of my long-awaited bonding with another I could not see that approaching within the brightness was a scorching fire.

That of the transcendence to another reality.

So, next day the miracle disintegrated! The x-ray XXA type passed automatically into another era; that of the countdown. Downwards to Hades... The spaceship of the most modern technology did not land on the sea and it exploded in the air and its parts flew in the air and dispersed in the universe.

Andre threw the x-rays on the kitchen table and said:

"I have cancer," while looking straight into my eyes to gauge my reaction.

"Stop kidding," I told him with a trembling hope that he was, in fact, joking; for it was practically part of our daily life. It had been an important source of nutrition and diversion amidst the routine demands of stressful urban life. So I desperately preferred that he was joking. Our life was practically a cartoon reel that had suddenly become a distorted caricature of itself.

"I'm not joking," he said seriously. Handing me the x-rays, he uttered, "Look for yourself."

I looked at the x-rays with trembling hands, still feeling the fluttering of an increasingly forlorn hope in my bosom that this might all be a performance of sorts. But unfortunately that fragment of hope vanished.

Suddenly life had been overturned, and was resolutely face-down. The shelter of love and affection that we both had erected started to crumble. Ready for formal demolition was Andre and I. What an irony!

"Hello, can you hear us? We are breaking doooooown....!"

I shouted but nobody could hear me. Nobody.

My exasperation was lost in the universe, into the huge deathly silence of hospital waiting rooms, operating rooms, intensive care stations, all gas chambers of frustration and decomposition. My thoughts ran to cruel comparisons with German history, but it was history that was at fault. These events comprised my 'own' story with my beloved husband, both of us ascending our own Golgotha, burdened with the wooden cross, sweating blood.

Poor supplicant, climbing up a hill in order to be crucified, a titanic preface to the act of execution!

Why must the journey end so painfully? Why should we not leave this world with the simple exertion of a breath just like the way we entered it? With a breath only. Commemorated with tears, a blowing of the wind. What sins are we obliged to repay for at the point of departure? The audacity to have transcended ourselves!?

Why not? Flights of fancy are a necessity to evade the mundane and the mediocre.

Not over exceeding the limits. That was our mistake. We had not perceived the limitations that constrained us, thus exceeding them. Consequently, the meaning of this oversight that is so common to us all is that we, as human beings, will be never free. What liberty have we gained since we are unable even to choose our death, to have a control over our passage from life?

Nonsense!

Why? As I had for innumerable times in my life, I was wondering yet again, "Why?"

Two years lasted his suffering. We felt like we were walking with a knife stabbed in our back. It had already gone through my chest and I felt it, I touched its projected edge. I touched it and I was bleeding with him; as I would be until we reached the end of that long journey.

What a journey! Strange and weird! Extremely slow at times and at the end so desperately fast! You feel so sorry as you finger the edges of distress. You cry for the pending kiss, the forthcoming good bye. You exist in madness and misery, mired in abjection because you have realized what a pathetic and insignificant facet of the universal causality.

How else can you describe death? It is exactly like love. Life and death united together. Life and death; birth and resurrection. There are no words left to describe the end. Only deathly silence. An immense silence... You get lost in an archipelago of annihilation, drifting in a rusted vessel of fate.

Higgledy-piggledy, counting down hours and minutes that have been stripped of their former meaning.

Down, down, always down, exactly like the run-up to a space launch.

10, 9, 8 7, 6, 5, 4, 3, 2, 1, lift-off!

The beginning of the end is always counted downwards. Why?

INSTEAD OF AN EPILOGUE

A stem-cell operation suddenly came across my mind; concerning me! That was the problem now. Me again on stage. This time, the play was distinctly dramatic, no trace of humor. I have been long accustomed to making fun of myself since I felt very strong and arrogant. By the time Andre passed away and during his treatment in the hospital I had started to submerge deep inside myself.

For me, getting elegantly dressed, carefully putting on make-up, my eyes, and my hair was pointless. What for? To visit him in the hospital? Sometimes I did not wish to pass through the hospital door. I felt so scared, weak and insecure. From the outset of Andre's treatment I was fighting with the doctors who often refused my involvement in my husband's medical treatment; later on I resigned from every fight, from every battle, from every struggle due to my collapse from sorrow and distress. I found myself always in possession of my psychoanalyst's calling card.

After so many years since my mid-twenties, I felt like I had reverted to my past miserable state that was defined by self-pity.

Fate, according to me, was to blame for my destiny beneath a perpetual burden of sorts. During the fierce clarity of the moment, when Andre's life force waned, I hated me again and self-pitied me! I looked at Selfie and did not fancy it all! The heavy cocktail of medications to which he was subjected in his final few months precluded my sharing anything with him about these troubles. And during the increasingly few periods that he was lucid, I did not dare add my gloom to his adversity.

I had to carry on with my heavy load ALONE. That was the only way. I shared my despairing Selfie only with my best friends, but they were all in Greece.

After so many years of ample and sustaining injections I felt I had returned to the point just prior to my self-esteem. Yes, I felt useless, without any interests and initiative, without any meaning in an unjust life, mostly ugly, not attractive at all, a "cripple" again, especially because my listless state left me limping more than ever. Andre's pending death entailed the loss of my self-esteem and self-confidence. Indeed, it was very strange.

That is when an article about a stem cell operation in a scientific journal attracted my attention and I thought right away it would be a good chance for me to recover from my sorrow and distress, frustration and isolation. None of those adjectives can describe and express my feelings.

Indeed, there were no effective weapons to be used against the vanity and arrogance of Fate. Just like that, our life was turned upside down forcing me once more to stay there still on the ground.

Fate, a cold-blooded executioner!

Selfie, impotent and disposable!

I was searching like a maniac on the internet to discover everything possible about those stem cell operations, especially in America. Although those operations had very good results in England too, I preferred America more.

I wanted to get as far as possible away from Germany or Europe, since my husband there had been treated and tortured — a judgment of mine that is unabashedly attributed to my stereotypically "hot" Mediterranean mentality.

I had the feeling that after a while the doctors had given up on Andre as a human and were interested mostly in him as a very special and exceptional medical case. The large and small bowel have been removed and he lived for seventeen months since then on a total parenteral nutrition.

One day the Dr. Professor who was attending Andre invited me into his office and told me:

"You know, Mrs. Zavolia, your husband is prepared to take his last trip. We are almost at the end, and since there is no need to hide the truth from you, we are very much interested in a unique medical opportunity his case presents for us. We would like to take this opportunity to conduct further research which might ultimately provide some hope to the multitude of other patients in similar circumstances. I am obliged to ask for your permission for further research on this subject. It will take us some time to perform but when we are ready he will be at your disposal for burial services. I think you've chosen the crematorium..."

Uppss! What a torture!

It was not easy at all! I followed their instructions word by word and I was relieved that everything at last came to an end.

The end! Sometimes unbearably slow and other times mercilessly fleeting.

There is no need to talk about it… I think I've spoken my last words. Andre's soul sailed away, opening itself like a billowing sail, borne by his lost youth, heading for the southern sun he had always relished. The tempting south of our dreams and journeys; his whole life has been an adventurous long journey to the south.

"Me, the northern guy loves the south," he would say. "The sun, the light, that intense brightness in everything, the blue sky, the sea… It's amazing how all these natural elements affect people's feelings and mood. That's one of the reasons that people in the south rarely commit suicide unless there is a very serious psychological problem. How can you commit suicide and abandon all those miracles of nature? Probably the fact that they don't drink so much when compared to their northern neighbors is a contributing factor too, since there is far less compulsion driven by the northern climate and industrial alienation. The southerner drinks out of joy of life and the persistence of friends; often akin to children that never want to grow up."

However, I, the southern as well, had never enough of his love, too.

Only ten years! Our relationship had been such a short voyage; it had melted with the first snow… In the beginning of January, he wished me a "Happy New Year" and promptly departed. Fading away, he receded to another world without even a farewell.

He had been the best injection I had ever had...! Such a fantastic restorative injection before vanishing into oblivion. What a pity!

Well, dreams are not to satisfy your hunger. Whatever you love you always have a shortage of. Love compels you to thirst and hunger, leaving you sick more often than not. However, the lack of love has the same effect on you. Who can live without love? And who can leave earthly love without a kiss?

I soon found myself looking desperately for new injections again. My injections! Where are my injections? I was almost shouting.

"Where are those miraculous injections?"

I was asking all over.

Some people are looking for their pills, their narcotics, and I was looking for my injections. I had been so dumb to think that I had been cured.

Let's start from the beginning again! In the wake of Andre's passing I was lost once again in an archipelago of solitary meaninglessness. I lost my self-esteem and confidence, ever searching like a junkie to find magic injections. I just wanted to take a trip, get my dose, and take another trip, become a tripper like all hurt people are travel, descending into limbo and cruelty, into hallucinations and lassitude, into that fictional delirium drugs usually create. Yes, if I had drugs I would have surely taken them! When you are desperate it is so easy to transcend the present world and find yourself stranded in another.

In which world though? Which is the real one? The one that hurts you less, I'd rather say.

I, a badly paid teacher by the Greek Ministry of Education, packed my memories and images and left all my burdens in my Berlin wake. How could it be otherwise? How can somebody start a new life if one hasn't already packed well away the discomforts of the old one? You have to take out the trash first! A new life has to be completely clean from pain and tears.

I licked my finger and turned the page. I started a new life!

I, Zavolia, was repatriated.

I stepped again on the familiar earth of Greece and felt somehow regenerated for simply having done so. My dreams and expectations! How should they be paid? With monthly installments or in cash? No more debts.

A respectable arrangement of my sentiments.

That is the epilogue of the story and the prologue, too. A prologue to the efforts of a person trying to approach her fellow Greeks.

An epilogue though to the herein chronicle of a "special" person different from the "normal ones," of a human being not satisfying society's required standards. Of a human being compelled by circumstance to transcend and overcome her otherness as a means not only of survival but of social recognition and personal fulfillment.

That is me, indeed — Zavolia — and I will end up my story here by causing no more trouble and making no more fuss about it. After all, it was only an impulse to identify myself as a Selfie facing each other. It is like dancing or exercising. You may sprain your ankle or even break it during moving delirium. Nothing is steady or fixed. Like in life! Mostly unpredictable!

My return to Greece was not easy at all but my experience in my homeland was unlike those of the past. I was completely transformed. I cared about little else other than accomplishing my plans and goals. I claimed my rights as a handicapped person, being persistent, insistent, persuasive, unhesitating and occasionally unscrupulous when necessary. To threaten Gods and Demons without shame and mercy.

I took advantage of my lame leg to enter formerly restricted areas and succeed. I should not omit to say that our public system now has been upgraded in a way with special laws concerning people with "special needs," just because a lot of funds were given by the European Committee to the Greek government to specifically target that way our mob and bandits — the politicians — instead of "misplacing" funds finally reformed and enacted the law. The general improvement of the state of "special needs" citizens over the last few decades is a manifest reality. Though low developed, we belong now to the European Union! Through the new laws and agendas of this supranational organization, the rights of handicapped people have been protected and projected into the routine functioning of almost all public services.

We have been modernized in a way in order to impress the rest of the world who stereotyped us as loafers, gangsters, bandits and generally untrust-worthy. Not us, our politicians I mean, though we carry a great part of the responsibility with our vote!

I have refined my circus tricks in order to survive. Selfie and I, a funny clown with a red nose and psychedelic clothes covering my deformity, I command the whole performance from the beginning to the end, and then I perform my somersaults, enticing my audience with my frenzied pace. In that way, I ingratiate them to me due to the obstacles to my fluid performance, obstacles purchased with dried blood and many tears. In the beginning my jokes were too serious for some people.

THE EXPERIMENT

My second trip to the USA was not the same. Then I was sixteen, now I was sixty. A great difference and a big gap between the ages.

Compromising is not that simple. It takes time and energy.

My age was not the obstacle on my way. The problem still existed; I felt healthy and young to make a new experiment. I was determined for the big transform. Why not?

Beautifully transformed ladies are still unable to deal with their personal experiences and complexes, resulting in operation after operation in search of a renewed aesthetic! Yet, no remedy can heal their traumas. They have disembarked from the train of real life, expecting the next one to promptly follow in its wake.

It rarely shows up.

My own train came on time during my later years. The trauma that preceded it was the consequence of a death — not only a physical one but a mental one as well. It occurred to me to discover what it would be like to look and live as I was "normal and healthy," to walk without limping and rapidly tiring; to jump, to nimbly climb the stairs without scarcely a care; to enjoy the beauty of nature without leaning on a tree or a cane; to indulge in any sport I liked; to feel physically capable; in other words, to feel ready to advance forthrightly into the new world arrayed before my eyes. This is what matters now!

In light of my trauma, why shouldn't I appeal to the services of the national health system and the support of Social Security?

Selfie, in America again, after so many years. What an experience! On my own, and with my own money; supported by the acquired wisdom of my life. It was an experimental surgery by the Medical University Clinic. I was consulted and thoroughly informed of the consequences of the pending operation. As though I was hypnotized, I did not listen to anything the doctors told me, resigning myself to a new beginning and routinely consenting to their propositions.

Selfie, the best medical test animal ever.

What an animal, a real beast!

Nothing to lose, much to win; much like gambling. A good poker game with the red jack threatening my future and the good king sweetening my dreams.

"After all, it's only a game!" I secretly shouted primarily for my own benefit.

I should come up for the hospital expenses while the doctor's fee were to be borne by the hospital. A good business deal. Like in any other country outside Greece, at least you were afforded the opportunity to succeed. The operation would be an exotic gift of sorts to my new life as a mature woman. The best gift ever. An opportunity to explore the world that others readily enjoyed, an opportunity to be experienced before the conclusion of my life. Why not? We come here in order to learn; yes, to learn mostly about that part of the inner self that perpetually remains aloof. Most people come to their end without ever having known anything about themselves or the purpose of their existence.

I was staying at the best hotels in New York while visiting the most prominent hospitals, foundations and institutes that boasted a rich research background in stem cell operations. It was just me, all alone, without friends. Just I and Selfie!

I wondered as to who was going to inform my people in Greece if I did not survive the operation? In light of this possibility, I was obliged by hospital official to provide detailed information about relatives and so on. In light of the experimental nature of the treatment and operation and any dire complications that they might entail, the hospital needed the consent of my "next of kin." Lacking relatives, the hospital would have to bear the responsibility for choices made. This, they wanted to avoid, but in that instance who is going to prosecute them?

The procedure consistent of the transfusion of stem cells from a donor embryo into my blood. "I am grateful to you my friend; you give me the chance to explore another dimension of life," I told that microscopic being. I and Selfie awaiting a miraculous coexistence. Will one being function for the benefit of the other or the opposite? In a few days I would find out.

Lying in the hospital bed in a famous New York Hospital, I am looking forward to the great day under the gaping surgical lamps. It is the first time in my life I am not afraid at all, of anything, either operations, or injections. I had so many of the latter that it had little effect on me. On the contrary I become very impatient to move forth. I am curious to see the results. I want it fast, painless, and effective.

All the preparations are complete and the next step is my transfer into the secretive recesses deep within the hospital where all that magic will take place. Indeed it is a mysterious procedure how science progresses and makes people's life more comforting and respectable. All people should have the right to such magical procedures but most cannot afford it. Education and health should be free for all. However, they are both purchased by the devil!

The guinea pig, me, is in its cage, pacing, waiting for the door to open and to be pushed a little beyond the frontier of medical knowledge. During this crucial time I am reading and thinking a lot, watching TV sometimes to relax and fall asleep. Time needs time! Most of the people fight with the time as though there is no time at all.

The winner will become the loser and the defeated will become the winner. The terms have been overturned. "The day after" will not be the same any more, no matter what the result of the operation is.

Finally they came to take me...

When I opened my eyes, I had an intensive sensation of relaxation, a heavenly comfort. I was lying alone in a white sterilized room. Nobody was around, only the humming technology at the edge of my bed monitoring my life force. Positive and impressive, they sounded!

I immediately blinked my eyes repeatedly, as though I distrusted my sight. I tried to move my hands and then legs. Then I heard a voice coming, as if, from nowhere.

"Well, how do you feel?"

"Like coming back from Heaven," I said, turning my head to see whoever was addressing me.

"That's a good feeling, eh?" It was a man's voice, a good-looking man's voice dressed up in hospital white. "You will be in Heaven for a while still," he added.

"Do you mean I will pass away?" I joked.

"'Live' in Heaven, I said. Not 'move' to heaven."

"What is the next step?"

"For you to get up and take some good and steady steps."

"Like a baby taking its first steps?" I asked him laughingly. "Or an adult suffering from arthritis?"

"Whatever," he answered calmly and took my hand to measure my pulse, I suppose.

"My recovery. How long will it take?" I asked.

"It depends!"

"On what?"

"On you, on your will."

"Meaning what?" I asked again.

"Let's say willingness to walk the way you want."

"I don't believe in miracles."

"What I meant is your willingness to believe in miracles," he said smiling, at last. "Besides the very fact that you took the decision to go through this experience means that you believe in miracles."

"Yes, I have to admit that. My whole life has been shot as if in a miraculous circus!"

"What a movie, eh?" he exclaimed. "I would like very much to watch it. Where is it showing?"

"You'll have a good chance to watch it. It's still running, don't worry!" I told him.

"I am looking forward to it, I can't wait."

Looking him straight in the eyes, I earnestly asked.

"How long do I have to stay here — because I don't want to miss it myself?"

"A couple of days… hours… it depends. But you are the starring actress. You should have been invited to the premiere, don't you think?"

"I will be invited to the next premiere. It will take place in a few days, as you said."

"Will that be the second or third part of a trilogy perhaps?"

"Trilogy will be after death, like we say 'BC'. In that case we'll say 'BZ' as for Zavolia," he said enjoying the wordplay immensely.

The doctor seemed to be very smart.

"You are a very good player, Zavolia. So, the answer to your question is: It depends."

"On what?" I asked again.

"I've already told you."

"It doesn't make any sense. But — what the hell — I'll take it for what it is," I said.

"That's a good girl."

"A good lady… Certainly somewhat older than a girl," I smiled and studiously took note of his reaction.

"We've done our best. Your body will take the final decision. Talk to it and welcome the new plasma with gratefulness. It really is worth it."

"I've been doing that constantly the last many years. I think we have a very good relationship, I and Selfie. The photo of myself! We understand each other very well. We have reconciled with each other for years now. It was only a matter of curiosity at this point to find out how 'normal' people live."

Suddenly the words were flowing more glibly than ever, as though I were mute and had just found my voice, as though I had passed away and had miraculously just returned from heaven or hell. Whatever!

"You don't mind publishing your case, the positive outcome of stem cells in curing polio in the best scientific journals? Do you? You soon very well might be giving speeches all over the world to assure the multitudes of 'Doubting Thomases.'"

"'Doubting..?'"

"Yes, those with obsessed contradictions, objecting to such kinds of interferences and challenges," he said. He was a fantastic speaker. I started fancying him a lot though it was hardly the time or place for flirting.

Curious, I asked, "What do you mean by 'interferences'?"

"Interference means that transfusion with the neon plasma you received. That is a great scientific achievement and most 'Doubting Thomases' contest this approach; they say the transfusion should have been comprised of your own stem cells. Otherwise it has no effect."

"Who are these people that oppose your approach?" I inquired, being extremely interested in this medical dispute. But the dispute implicitly affirmed the substantial possibility that the procedure might fail. I suddenly became very irritated and stressed.

The doctor did not seem to notice my discomfort. "There is a great conflict and competition between the colossal pharmaceutical companies. They fight for the 'lion's share' of the rewards and unfortunately against the welfare of society."

I liked him a lot. He seemed to be a magician of sorts.

"How could I have used my own stem cells since there was not such a medical procedure?"

"That is what I mean. What we've done here applies not only to the future but to the present as well. It's only that in the future it may be easier and more applicable. That's why you have been requested for forthcoming experimental stages as well."

"Yes, I know. You indicated something to that effect in your website. I applied to that, too. I thought that was my big chance for a repeat performance as an experimental beast, first for myself and then for the welfare of the people."

"Surely you are not a beast. Do you like characterizing yourself so? You underestimate yourself, you deserve better. So no 'experimental beast.' In your case I would say 'a sweet little mouse.'"

The attractive doctor was become more so to me.

"And to tell you something else," he added. "Your volunteering in that project is very important; it helps our experiments in this field. Just think how many diseases can be cured through these transplants. Let's say cancer, eh?" He was expecting an answer from me but I was growing fatigued.

"I am so proud of me!" I said to him. I sort of fancied him, I think. He was such an intelligent person, a brilliant doctor maybe, a genteel personality. Who knows? Middle forties, I guessed. Good looking and neat.

He took on a serious tone and proclaimed: "You know what? I think it's great to encounter people who are willing to improve themselves, to make the best out of their circumstances because they love and respect themselves."

"I love me, I love Selfie, indeed, and that's why I take good care of me.

"It seems so, we figured that out immediately after the first time we met you. Normally we do not transplant people who have very low self-esteem. We need optimistic and courageous people with faith and the willingness to invest some confidence in our efforts. Believe me, it does not work out when the patient is not persuaded that it is going to be effective and relatively successful."

"From what I've heard and seen I am the right person to be used for this experiment."

He regained his casual demeanor and smiled. "I think so, too."

"You know what, my dear doctor. The only thing that is disagreeable about all this so far is staying alone in this room. I don't like at all being alone."

"Today you are going to relax and rest, dream and smile to yourself, and then sleep again. Although tomorrow is another matter."

"How can I relax after such a conversation? I'm rather excited by it," I said, almost giggling.

"Now I'm leaving so you can relax. Again, tomorrow will be another day."

"If I survive, you mean?"

"I think you can pretty well depend on that much despite the reality that every procedure includes an element of life or death. You'll have plenty of company today, since every hour or so one of the doctors of my team will be paying you visits, telling you stories about the bit of history that is unfolding here."

"Was this all only a story, you mean?" I asked.

"Of course, a science fiction story," he joked, simultaneously pressing my hand.

"Are you leaving now?"

"I'd prefer not to, but I have to make space for the next doctor to come. But I'll come again at midnight when all the ghosts appear."

"Will you be one of them?" I joked.

"I'll become one just only to check on your reactions and scare you a bit."

"Then we'll shoot a terror film!"

"No, we'll shoot a happy film," he said.

"Well, well... you talk in such riddles."

"Probably because I am a riddle myself."

"Of course, why shouldn't you be? No objection," I added.

"Now, I have to go and I'll send in the next doctor," he proclaimed.

"I welcome whoever is next but I particularly enjoyed your company, doctor."

"Thank you. I'll keep that in my mind before making my next visit."

"Keep it and think about it," I said, with more boldness than I intended.

"See you later alligator," he said, waving good bye.

A near continuous stream of ten doctors soon followed that lasted until midnight, each with a particular interest that surfaced after the conventional pleasantries. Some of them were interesting, some boring, some very formal, some extremely amusing with a very good sense of humor. I was not bored at all, the time seemed to pass rapidly. By the end of the stream of visits I felt the fatigue of a ten-hour workday.

I had almost fallen asleep when I heard a knock on the door that was located somewhere behind my bed. During the whole time, I had not moved at all, lying in bed, no food, no drink; it was as if I was a neglected plant potted in place, a ward of the humming technology. Was I in an intensive care unit? There had hardly been any time to ask exactly where I was located in light of the stream of purpose-driven doctors, supporting staff, nurses, assistants, etc.

A voice from somewhere behind me softly stated: "I won't disturb you, only wish you a good night and a relaxing break from the procedure."

It was the voice of my good doctor. Instantly appearing at my side, he enquired, "How did you get along with the visitors?"

"Very well, I suppose. Were there any complaints amongst them about an odd and demanding patient?"

"Not at all," he said heartily. "On the contrary. All of them have the best opinion of you. They compare you to an angel assisting our team's good work."

"Really? I would have no objection to developing a good reputation in the hospital, my dear doctor. Let's find a good title for my new film, a new blockbuster."

"Another film?" he asked me.

"I've told you already, in the morning, at noon, I have no sense of time in here. There is a good film with me in the starring role that is already playing. You seemed to be very interested in that film."

"Oh, yes, I apologize. Yes, I have to watch that film. I'm a bit confused like yourself. You see, you're an impressive patient, an exciting patient. That's why I wish you the best luck, Zavolia, you deserve it."

"Thank you, thank you a lot. But to tell you the truth, even if nothing — let us cross our fingers — works out, well... the experience itself would have made it worth it. The journey matters... not the destination. And I happen to be rather fond of journeys, however long they might be. I live to explore and nothing else. That is why I've undertaken so many fascinating trips in my life. So far, as I lay in this bed, I'm impressed, too. Honestly!" For his benefit, I closed my eyes as if I was spiritually travelling at that very moment.

"The trip matters and nothing else. The people who dare not go on that trip is a very unfortunate soul indeed." He paused and then added: "I'd better leave you to rest in peace."

"I do not wish to rest in peace but in war!" I declared. "I am not really sleepy. This discussion with you is very effective, honestly, the best medication I could have received. Perhaps a remedy for the future." I found myself flirting with him without shame.

"Only ten minutes," he uttered. "Because I have been rather taken in by my own patient's conversation that I too do not wish to say good night."

I was laughing again. "You mean, 'eternal good bye; lying in peace'?"

"Fortunately or unfortunately," Dr. Simon stated. "I have become part of your life; my work an element of your body. I am attached to you and there is no way back. I transfused elements into your blood that will have to be attended to closely and professionally for years, my dear. Even if I wished so, I can't get away from you. There is no separation from each other in our case, not even a chance of a divorce, like the Catholics, we have to stay together as long as we live. Only death will separate us." he said very earnestly.

"Wooow!" I exclaimed. "You've instantly become a doctor for life, right?"

"Or a man for life," he retorted. "Don't forget I am of the male sex."

"Yes, I can see that," I affirmed. "But I cannot confirm it, ha, ha!"

"Unless you want to," he said calmly.

"That is no official enquiry, doctor."

"It's a part of the whole game, the whole procedure," he added.

"Good, then I'll accept it that way."

"Anyway," he said.

"You are doing a great job, here, sir," I seriously stated.

Reaching over and pressing my hand, he added.

"We do our best, my lady."

"What is the plan for tomorrow?" I asked.

"Let's leave it a surprise. If you need something press the button for the nurse. Ok?"

"And a last but not least question, Professor. I've heard you are the head professor of the clinic. Isn't that right? Where is this room? Is this an intensive care unit?"

"Yes, but in space, my dear lady. Good night!"

"You may have been right, a science fiction story, isn't it?"

"Have a good night," he said, disappearing out the door.

When I woke up the next morning it was as if the room had been heavenly illuminated; ice white cold to the eye. There was an intensive smell of medicine in the room, but I could not identify it. I tried to sit up but soon relented and rung the bell for the nurse. But the most peculiar thing was the utter lack of bodily demands upon my will. I was neither hungry, thirsty or in need of the bathroom. "I may be in outer space," I thought. "I may be captured in a huge space ship where everything is precisely monitored, nourished and instantly indulged. I may be a robot or something like that. I need a mirror to look at myself."

"Good morning," said a cute nurse with a fresh smile. "How are you this morning?"

"I think I am fine; but quite frankly, I am not sure yet. Could you please help me with the bed? Is it possible to raise it a little bit?"

"Of course, of course, today it's allowed," she said.

"Can I have a mirror, please?"

"Of course, of course. Is there anything else you need?"

"I cannot exactly say 'if' I want something," I confessed. "I'm a bit confused."

"Don't worry. Give it some time and you will be fine. I have to prepare you for the doctors. They will be arriving soon." First she brought me the mirror I requested but she did not hand it over to me. She washed and cleaned me, combed my hair and put a new hospital gown on me.

"Here you are, beautiful lady," she said, matter-of-factly handing me the mirror.

"Thank you, thank you."

I found myself to be very pale, as though they had drained my blood instead of infusing new blood. It scared me somewhat, but I overcame it. Maybe that small embryo that was the source of my new stem cells was suffering from leukemia and the disease was part of the infusion.

"Why do I look so pale?" I asked the nurse, as though her assurance would be comforting.

"It's completely normal after the procedure you've undergone, Mrs. Zavolia," she said simply. When her preparations were complete, she promptly excused herself and left.

I was left alone again in that cold room and I took account of its every detail. Very simple in colors and style. There was not a sound to be heard, nothing save the quiet operation of the monitoring devices. There was no furniture besides my bed and the instruments, not even a side table, not a chair. Nothing. So I suppose I was in an intensive care unit or some sort.

I managed to turn around and finally saw that door. It was the only door. Not even a bathroom door. I wanted to get out of that room, right away, it scared me. It looked like a luxurious grave where one could lie in bed and expire in peace. What a film!

"I would like to get out of this tomb-like room," I said to my friend Dr. Simon who came to visit me first.

"Be patient a little. Tomorrow you will be transferred to another room, to another world."

"I hope not the underworld," I quipped.

"I see that you are in good spirit. Let me look at your leg." He uncovered my bed sheets and touched my leg with his magic hands; it was a soft touch that scarcely seem to serve any exploratory purpose before laying the sheet once more over the leg. He smiled. "Let's take our time."

"How long do I have to stay immobile like this?"

"During midday I'll come again and we will see. Today you won't have so many visitors other than me and my assistants."

Despite having great expectations and pangs of impatience, I did not comment. I had already been informed of the operation itself. It would take time for the results. Nor were those results consistently apparent, often getting worse before improving and vice versa. The recovery would require a stolid constitution and a deep fund of patience to call upon. I did not want to force anything.

My languid morning eyes met those of the doctor.

"Patience and forbearance had been a central theme of my life. What would be the purpose of a change at this point?"

"Change should be forthcoming, believe me, my small Greek lady. You came all the way from Greece to find good fortune in America. It's the least we can do," he said and pressed my hand again, the one with the intravenous tubes.

"I found my good fortune in America when I was sixteen, almost at the beginning of my life, and I'm sure I'll find my good luck again here at the twilight of my life. America, America has been a wonderland for me. I got what I asked for. I am grateful to America, and I have a great respect for its people and great progress in all fields, though my political views are totally divergent. Its policies scare me, not the country. Sometimes I've wished the global influence of this country was radically curtailed, for its own good."

"We'll talk politics later. Then we will have lunch together somewhere and talk about everything that concerns or does not concern us."

"I'll be looking forward to that day, sir," I said obediently.

He promptly became the professional scientist as any personal affect that had been on his face instantly fell away. "I'll see you soon, have a good day."

I was left all alone again to count the tiles on the wall.

Gone with the wind a couple of days later, exactly like the first one and there was no alteration in movements or locations. Nothing altered on the fourth, fifth or sixth day, and soon I was not counting anymore. During all those days though I felt like being paralyzed although I could move my legs and hands the same way like before; In bed only not standing and so on.

Finally the big day came!

First, my friend, Dr. Simon, the great Professor, came in the morning with his assistants and declared triumphantly.

"Today is the big day! You will be transferred to another room, a normal room, let's say, isolated again but not excluded from the rest of the world. It's a single room again but from today on you should live like a normal person.

He unplugged one by one all the support equipment before removing the intravenous tubes from my arms. He had set me free and I was most grateful.

"At last, I regain my personal freedom, too," I said laughingly. "No longer suspended in those thousands of cables and tubes, feeling my very life was dependent on them. This is a big step."

"Now, next," he said to me. He took both of my legs and let them hang off the bed, preparing me rise to my feet.

"Put your legs down and try to stand up," he gently ordered.

I did what he said.

Such a fantastic feeling; to be touching the ground again with two steady legs! I felt weak but stable on two strong legs. However I did not move, dreading the very thought of sliding my foot along the floor. Being accustomed to falling in the past, and fearing that the failure to do so now signified failure, was a strong incentive for hesitation.

"Come on, Zavolia," he encouraged me, while holding my arm. "Try to walk now, try to walk, slowly. I'll support you. Don't be scared. Come, come, that's a good girl, a good baby, one by one, don't stiff up."

One by one, one by one, one by one, my first last steps in life. Step by step I entered the world of "normal people." Step by step I entered the world of the "healthy ones." Up to that point these worlds had been restricted areas.

I was walking well, normally, without any effort; of course I was limping but I did not need any support. My weak leg had suddenly become strong. My thoughts ran to the miracles of Jesus Christ, the miracles I'd been watching in movies during Easter with my father and brother, those movies where all the paralyzed people of the world rose from their beds and started to walk, the blind ones who started to see.

I was walking alone, unsupported, not even the assuring touch of my own hand upon my upper thigh.

I could not believe my eyes! My own body... independent. I did not dare ask, "How do you feel, babe?" I was as I was always meant to be.

"I can't believe it," I exclaimed as everyone smiled broadly. A young intern wept silently. A great sense of relief filled the room, a great emotion of accomplishment that even seemed to compel the cold walls to convey some semblance of warmth.

The disposition of Dr. Simon was one of complete formality, allowing no sentiment to escape his reserve; very professional, not at all enthusiastic. He was closely studying my reactions. Addressing them specifically.

"I can easily walk, no doubt, it seems so. But it's not so easy to say whether that is real or not; it's either a miracle or a demon's trick. I can't say how I feel. That too will come, isn't that so, Professor?"

"You take as much time as you wish, my dear," he casually said, before tenderly adding, "Now, if you return and sit on the bed, lie down, and you will be taken to your new environment. We'll pay you our next visit there. We'll follow you in other words, little Greek Zavolia."

There had been a clear element of affection in his tone, but he quickly expunged it, not wanting to sound sentimental in front of his subordinates. He was the famous Professor, after all!

I did whatever he said.

Overwhelmed by the immediacy of a manifest "new life," I lay quietly in bed. What were the ritual expectations and practices now living in the world of the "normal ones"? Although a new world where I might ostensibly be free of the reflexive rejection that I had so commonly received I was still mistrustful of the new social landscape within which I found myself. I needed my own time and my own space to make my definitive entry the new world and conclude a treaty of some sorts with its inhabitants. Would I reconcile with my former persecutors! I was also afraid that the new miracle would be dissolved by daylight. I had learned to trust only me. I suspected my enemies might be waiting for me outside the hospital to attack my brand new leg.

My leg seemed new to me after injecting those miraculous stem cells but I was so terrified with my new mainstream identity.

"*Let it be,*" somebody whispered into my ear. "*Let it be....!*"

SELFIE AND I

Sweat all over, dripping like a broken pipe, wet drops rolling down my face on to clean bed covers, I was looking desperately for a hanky to stop the perspiration. Lying in the dark, I could not figure out where I was. I slid my legs out from under the covers and proceeded to the bathroom. When I started to walk I instantly realized that something was still wrong with me.

I looked for my doctor. Where was he?

"Hello, Professor, you are deluded. Do you hear me? You are deluded in your experiment! It has failed! There is no difference, no progress. I am the way I was. Can you hear me? Your transplant, how do you call it, your 'transfusion,' has failed. There was a big mistake of some sort. Unfortunately I was not the best experimental animal for this great achievement.

"You failed. And I have failed right along with you since nothing has changed. I am walking the same way. I am getting tired. I need a support for my leg. It was ultimately only an illusion, a fake, eh? That's all right. I freely volunteered for this throw of the dice. I knew it from the very beginning that it may not work out. I won't regret it! Nevertheless, I still went on the most fascinating trip ever. I traveled with you for a while and it was fantastic, so exciting. A miracle late in life. What? In my sixties? Who can earnestly expect miracles at this age?"

"Stop it, you idiot! Stop grumbling. You are so miserable. Miracles can happen every day, every single moment no matter who or what you are. You know that better than everybody. Your life was full of miracles simply because you yourself fashioned them. You have made up your own myth and fairy tale in order to make the best out of your life and you have experienced the most and the best. Don't talk nonsense then! Look at you, babe. You look great but you do not have enough money to go on with that whole operation. It will cost a lot of money, and don't be silly to think that there are sponsors who will help you finance such an experiment. What would be their profit to make you able to walk like everybody else? You had better go and look for some other source of support on your own. Otherwise, forget it. If you can dream a miracle, you can make a reality.

"Yes, you may be right, Selfie. I am talking to you because you are the only one who really understands me, the only one who is willing to walk the point, breaking down walls before me. You are unbelievable. You are great. You are something very special. I admire you more than anyone else, and I think that you have been my best friend doing your best for me. I really appreciate it. Selfie, you are valuable and most precious. I wouldn't trade you for anything in the world!"

"You are flattering me, my boss, you know I don't like compliments. However I appreciate it a lot. Thank you!"

"That's the only truth, believing in Selfie, working out all my problems with Selfie, find a way out through Selfie, why shouldn't I respect you and praise you, eh?"

"Eh, eh, eh, I don't know why..."

"Come on now. Tell me. What am I going to do? I had a fantastic dream that awakened me when I really needed a change. That was it! But it stopped being wonderful, instantly transforming into a nightmare now. What I had in the past I still have it and nothing has changed that. But you know what? I do not care anymore! Why should I? I had thousands of those injections and they were very effectively on me. Why shouldn't I just take another one now and stop worrying about excessively colorful dreams that are gone with the wind? The game is over!"

"What, another injection again?"

"A sedative to make me forget about this exploded dream — a false vision that I was completely cured and physically rehabilitated; a false vision that meant that I would no longer have to keep on living like I had been. Over with it! So, get me one good shot now. I think I need an overdose, even though it might kill me. An injection without an expiring date so that I can call upon it any time I want."

"Yes, boss."

"And something else too. After all, it was only dream. It was so real and vivid that I'm still in a state of excitement, without any fear. For a brief moment I walked like a normal person. And believe me, it was such a gorgeous feeling, it was great, however brief. It was an unprecedented feeling in my life, and I think it was very good to have the chance to have that sensation.

"Nothing has really changed; I am still crippled, disabled, and the older I become, the more my energy and strength abandon my body. Whatever might be the results of this attempt at a new start, I'm still optimistic with respect to this procedure. The truth is that there have been real miracles in this particular field of medical technology. Where should I find the money necessary to finance it? Do you know anybody who can support me?

"Now is the only thing I am concerned with at the moment. I am yearning for a real dream come true!"

"Yes, you are right."

"You little fool. That is the only thing you have to say? That I am right? Of course I'm right. You know what? I'll sell my house to fund the operation. That's it! I think I've got it. I won't need a house anymore since I'll be traveling around with my personal airplane. I hate flying but I'll overcome it. I'll be constantly on the move for more excitement, more learning, more adventure, more of whatever I need. So I am leaving!"

"Going where? You must be out of your mind again!"

"To list my home in the classifieds as well as on the internet. A real estate, for my 'real' state! What do you think?"

"I don't think!"

"Think then. Do you have another idea, perhaps?"

"Yes, don't forget to take me with you, too."

"How can I live without you, Selfie?"

"Yes, but in the past there have been times when you left me behind, when you've heartlessly abandoned me."

"Eh, come on now, that was long ago. Now, everything is on the move. Move now, move, we have to hurry up before we lose the train of sympathy!"

"The…, what?"

"The train of antipathy; two nice Greek words that are particularly fitting with respect to our relationship, too."

"Sympathy — antipathy"

"Ladies and gentlemen, the show has come to an end. I hope you enjoyed it and had fun with all our comic and tragic quirks and happenings. Now there will be a great parade of our whole circus; the wild animals, the beast tamers, the jugglers, and at the end, the acrobats. Give us a big and enthusiastic applause, please..! I think it is well-merited!"

Where do I belong now? I mean, in that traveling circus?

Well, you can classify me where I might properly fit in... *pshshsh...* I have told you from the very beginning, I am something very special and unique, and since I had those fantastic injections nobody can catch up with me!

Especially that last big shot in New York, being out of schedule, a decision impulsively made. I was so embarrassed! I have no idea how I can deal with it! I've jumped again. This time out of my former body and entered a brand new one, transformed by the best intents of new technology.

Even in my dreams I cannot predict my future. Surely I became a new beast in a savage world but who knows if I can accept my brand new identity? It may take some time to find out again, and I suppose I do not have the abundance of time I formerly had.

Should I enjoy it then?

"Take the last selfie and let's move. I had enough of those..."

About the author...

Elisa Iakovidou was born in Athens, Greece. She studied English and Greek Language as well as Literature at the Aristotle University of Thessaloniki and has been working as high school teacher at Greek public schools since 1983.
She has lived in the USA (1966–1967) and in Berlin, Germany (1990–2000), married to a German and teaching at the Greek High School in Berlin while at the same time being involved in cultural activities as member of the city's Greek Cultural Association.
She retired in 2010 and since then has been living in Mani, Peloponnese.
She has published many articles in magazines and newspapers in Greece and Germany, and has been nominated for some of her work in Greece.

Other publications:
    Anothefti Angalia [Pure Hug], Athens: Tsoukatou Publications, 2004
    Agrafo Dikio [Ethics in the Wild], Areopoli: Adouloti Mani, 2008
    Chrisi Laspi [Golden Mud], Athens: Anemos Ekdotiki, 2014 - First Prize in novel category, Panhellenic Writers Association

* Author seen on cover image

26981917R00113

Printed in Poland
by Amazon Fulfillment
Poland Sp. z o.o., Wrocław